Celestine Algorithms

Heavenly Destiny

By Dr. Gina Pazzaglia

Dedicated to my beloved children, grandchildren, and special friends, who gave me the time, understanding, support, and grace needed while writing this book, and to those who have suffered the effects of domestic violence...

May the words within these pages bring help and solace to their souls.

Preface

Sue is typically reserved and guarded as an adult; as a child she suffered abuse and neglect at the hands of her mother and "her men." Sue, abandoned by a loving father, unsure of his whereabouts or the reasons for his departure, is in a general ambivalence to men. However, in a short-lived love affair, she finds herself pregnant. Sue struggles with the same ambivalence regarding her unborn child. Determined for "Little One" to avoid the agony she experienced during her own upbringing, she determines to keep the secret of the baby's existence from the self-centered sperm donor, Jorge, as well as her own narcissistic mother.

Sue faces many issues related to betrayal and trust as she finds courage to stand up for herself. Meanwhile, Jorge, the father of the unborn child has to face his own demons and Sue distances him. He begins to recognize his own character defects similar to those of his father, a political power monger.

Both Sue and her abandoning father have haunting dreams of an Indian Princess who through her unusual aberrations weave them on a pathway of self-evaluation and courage. With her guidance, will they finally find themselves as well as each other?

The goal of this first book *Celestine Algorithms/Heavenly Destiny* is to entertain, as well as educate readers. Workbook materials are forthcoming, designed to further healing and acceptance in the hearts of those who have suffered the effects of domestic violence. Through a 12-step model process, the author guides the reader through provocative questions related to recognizing powerlessness, coming to acceptance, and addressing character deficits that potentially alter and define each person's destiny.

Table of Contents

CHAPTER 1

I don't care what happens later, Sue argues with herself. *This feels amazing.* She glances at his body in an attempt to convince herself to surrender to her inner longings... *and he is so gorgeous!* Closing her eyes, finalizing her internal argument, she whispers, *what a stress release.* She moans as she gives herself to him. In the recesses of her mind, Sue acknowledges she neglected contraceptives, but the drive and the deep urge overwhelm her usually responsible self. She surrenders to the moment with all of herself.

The blueprint matrix rapidly comes together. His moaning and thrusting, her grasping of his back, clasping of his shoulders, the joining occurs. The releasing, the traveling, and then, there is new life.

The next several weeks are a blur for Sue. She is mostly preoccupied with work, but manages to see Jorge, her hottie, on occasion. She desperately wants to make a significant impression with upper management. She has worked diligently to gain her current position at Kirby Vacuum Cleaner Company. Sue prepares by rehearsing in the bathroom one last time. Suddenly a violent surge hits her stomach. *Oh, you gotta be kidding!* She wipes her mouth after hugging the toilet for the last 5 minutes. Looking in the mirror, seeing her flushed face and feeling her disheveled appearance, makes her want to pick up her purse and briefcase, and head out the exit. She speaks calmly to herself, as she rinses her mouth out. She rummages in her purse and finds a couple of breath mints. She hopes they'll do the job and tells herself, *You will be fine. You can do this. Pull it together. It is probably just the sushi from last night.*

She readjusts her skirt and attempts to appear poised as she enters the conference room. She has worked too long to let a little nausea, a little bad food choice, affect her presentation.

"Sue, are you alright," Diane asks. Diane is Sue's colleague and confidant. She is the epitome of women's confidence, with her stark, spiky black hair and intense blue eyes. "You look almost green...like the color of your skirt," ... she chuckles. Sue puts a hand on her stomach, gently and with annoyance, "Yeah, I am sure I will be fine; just something I ate or drank last night." Diane's slight twinge of envy emerged, "Are you sure it wasn't what you and Mr. Cool did afterwards?"

The negative sensation abates and Sue completes her presentation. Realizing she hasn't eaten all day, Sue grabs a quick bowl of chicken noodle soup.

Sue is much happier, now that she believes her stomach virus is gone. Throughout the day, she is aware of a frightening thought looming in the back of her mind. She asks herself, *Am I pregnant?*

Her intuition knows the answer, but her logic contradicts it. She rationalizes, *we used protection, and I just had my period.* Then remembers, because she just had her period, and had been on birth control, she didn't think she needed extra precaution. Once again, her intuition tells her she needs to go to the store to pick up a pregnancy test. Surrendering to her insight, lying that she just needs some antacid, Sue swings by Allgreens the neighborhood pharmacy. She quickly finds herself facing a dizzying variety of tampons, sanitary pads, panty liners, and condoms. Then she spots it, a pregnancy test kit. Her hand trembles as she reaches for it. Her stomach churns and her heart pounds. Deep in her soul, she knows, *my life is about to change.*

The phone in her pocket chimes, "I am Woman," by Helen Reddy. It's Diane's theme song and she certainly knows how to roar. Distracted by the tune, Sue selects the cheapest pregnancy test, as well as a box of pads. She hopes, perhaps by the contradiction of the purchase, her body will respond to the larger box with a menstrual cycle.

"Hello, yes, I am leaving the store and picking up some womanly product," she says. "I haven't felt good, and I am about to start my cycle."

Diane clears her throat, "Hmm, I was wondering about that? Are you sure you're not pregnant? I was just wondering, since you were throwing up today and I remember you were on an antibiotic last month. Sometimes those affect the birth control..." There is silence, and Diane senses she needs to stop talking... Sue burst into sobs.

Surprised, Diane responds, "Sue, get a grip...jeez, what is wrong with you? Did Jorge stand you up for the evening?"

"No, but I am standing here with a pregnancy test kit in my hand," Sue sniffles. Her nose streams. Her beautiful, artful eye makeup runs in colorful lines down the side of her face to the rim of her lips, where they meet the snot. She instinctively licks her lips and tastes the salty, bitter tears.

Diane softens her strident tone. Despite her blunt style and sarcastic humor, she is extremely intuitive and enmeshed with those she allows in her sphere of influence. She asks Sue, "Are you gonna take the test when you get home? Do you want me to be there? I mean, you probably aren't, but just in case... I mean, I know that would be tough to take by yourself if you see the ominous plus sign."

Diane tries some mild humor, to lighten the tension. Sue didn't find her attempts funny. Her sobs begin again, convincing Diane that her friend would need her more than ever in the coming days.

She tells Sue, "I'll meet you at your house in an hour. I have to stop by the apartment and change into my workout clothes."

She hopes Sue did not pick up the sentiment, but tells herself, *I might have to work out enough for the both of us if this turns out as if I suspect it will.*

"Alright," says Sue. "What were you just thinking?"

"Nothing, just that... just I am happy to have gotten past that stressful presentation today," Diane lies. She senses that her bluff pacifies Sue, and that is what matters at this point.

Sue pays for her purchases and barely arrives at her car, when it happens again; she throws up right there in the parking lot. Sue is beginning to feel that old sensation of derealization. This experience changes Sue's perception of her external world and everything seems to slow down. The sensational event makes her surroundings seem unreal and Sue begins to lose track of time. She used to feel it often as a child, but believed that feeling was far behind her. She wipes her mouth with a paper towel found in her glove compartment... *What is happening to me?*

LIFE AS SUE KNOWS IT is changing. What we don't see, is the movement of Spirit, as she has released her magical touch from the celestials. More brilliant than the light, these swirls of energy are warm pools of radiance, which move fast, like fractal algorithms. These are shapes that continue dividing and replacing themselves in smaller versions of themselves. Sent, or should we say 'beckoned' by Source, (perhaps called God or Spirit); *Little One* swirls, moves and breathes new life.

The small and intricate Being is growing, and changing daily. The being gently floating unknowingly in the new home, left behind the heavenly existence into an unusual opulent environment. The new life feels the warmth and buoyancy with a sense of comfort and security. Then it happens; violent thrusts disturb the tranquility, sparks of energy disperse, replaced by sensations of discomfort. Sue pulls over her car, hangs her head out the window, and throws up once again.

Reflections

While driving, her thoughts drift back to high school. She avoided male attention. She had way too much of that growing up with her pervert stepfather. Diane was always chattering about some male or another, in fact she did plenty of looking for the both of them. Diane mentioned how gorgeous Jorge was, but Sue barely acknowledged the fact he was quite the stud. Other than the accidental run-in just a short while back, she wonders if Jorge had ever noticed her. Life is full of idiosyncrasies...

**

About 10 minutes later Sue turns into the driveway of her small, efficiency apartment. She looks up and is surprised and perplexed about how she managed to get home. She does not remember getting into the car, securing her seatbelt, and starting the engine. She sees the big Styrofoam cup with its straw but she does not remember driving to her favorite drive-thru and getting the Banana Blast sitting in her cup holder. She does taste the flavor of banana and sour stomach in her mouth. As she feels the first jolt of frozen banana slush...*I'm really losing it... Today ...meant to be the turning point in my career.* It isn't exactly a career. The job she has is not even close to the one she HAD dreamed of as a child. It is just the best she can get with only a GED and no college education.

Sue recalls waking up that morning; feeling a little tired, and attributed that to one of her wild nights with Jorge. She remembers looking in the mirror and feeling happy with herself. At the age of 20, maybe there are dark circles under her eyes sometimes, but her large, green, almond-shaped eyes are accentuated by the latest hairstyle. Her thick brown hair frames her jaw line and highlights her eyes.

Sue has some Seminole blood, evident in the olive tone of her face. She works hard to maintain a reasonably attractive figure. She does tend to thicken in the middle, but rigorous sit-ups and core exercises make her appear mostly muscular.

Reflections

Sue dropped out of high school to escape the conflicts in her mother's home. She is the oldest of three siblings, or rather half-siblings. They have different fathers.

Sue's stepfather was using, his hands on her way too much. Either he was using them to strike her across the face or to grab her arms. The worst was that he used his hands to touch her body. At first, she felt special. Her stepfather, Mark, changed his attitude and   stopped hitting her. Then, he started calling her into whatever room he was in to discuss with her what he should do to her little sister who would refuse to do homework. Sue had just turned 12 at the time.

She remembers very little about her biological father. He was a very handsome and rugged truck driver, who was at least one quarter Seminole. His black hair was long, and he wore it in a braid down his back. Her parents had her shortly after they were married. She remembers being five years old; it is her last memory of him. Her father lifted her up into his giant, 18-wheeler, strapped her in, and took her on an overnight trip with him. As they drove away from their house, Sue's mother was yelling and screaming at him to bring Sue back or she would call the police for kidnapping. Sue remembers being happy to leave her mother, and hoping she and her father would never return.

She remembers feeling unsafe with her mother since she was very young. She recalls that her mother would get so drunk she would not fix her anything to eat. She remembers, too, having to sit in a wet diaper for hours sometimes. Being only three, she had limited understanding of drunkenness, but she clearly remembers her mother staggering around the house and then passing out most of the day on the couch.

Sue vaguely recollects that last day she saw her father. That day she and her father returned from their trip. A police car stopped in front of the 18-wheeler and a female police officer unbuckled her and lifted her down from the passenger seat, while another officer clicked handcuffs around her father's wrists. She was terrified and screamed, "Daddy! Daddy!"

He called out to her, "Hachi, don't worry, I will come and get you."

The police officer, still holding her tried to console her and said, "Your mother will come to get you soon."

The words made Sue cry even louder. Her mother picked her up at the police station and when she secured her in her booster seat, she grabbed her and said in her loudest, harshest tone, "You are a BAD GIRL! Do NOT ever let me hear you say that name he called you again or I will spank your bottom with my biggest wooden spoon!" The police officer had apparently referred to Sue as Hachi when her mother came to pick her up.

Sue knew that was a special name her father gave her and her mother could not stand Sue loving her daddy. She resented feeling left out while they traveled. From then on, every time Sue asked her mother about the whereabouts of her father. Her mother scolded and humiliated her, until she felt she was worthless. Sue's mother told Sue her father was a criminal and would "do serious time" if he ever came around again. Sue did not understand what "doing serious time," meant, so she decided it had to do with the time it would take him to come back home. That never happened.

During her elementary school years, Sue often stayed awake at night, praying to the stars, (or whoever made them) to bring her father home. Sometimes she dreamed her father's truck transformed into a stallion with wings, and would swoop down, out of the clouds, and she sees herself transported with him to a faraway island. Sometimes at night, she would dream of angelic beings. One always looked like an Indian Princess who would tell her to have hope and be brave. Despite these small moments of peace and hope, Sue's heart and mind became colder and harder as the days passed into years. After a while, the dreams and visitations disappeared.

* *

Sue is unsure how long she has been sitting outside her apartment in her deep blue 2007 Ford Focus. The windows are down since it is early spring, but the other reason they are open is if Sue suddenly becomes ill on the way home, it will be easier to pull over and hang her head out the window to vomit, instead of having to take off her seatbelt, open the door, and step around the car.

She could have stayed in her driveway indefinitely if she had not felt a light tap on her shoulder that startled her out of her timeless and fruitless memories. She had been drifting through intermittent, intrusive images of a father who was now merely a shadowy figure in her history, and of a mother, who continues to spew relentless guilt tactics. Sue has worked very consistently at ignoring and resisting them both.

"What are you doing out here," Diane asks Sue, as she opens the door for her, grabs her arm, and assists her towards the stairwell to her apartment on the second floor.

Suddenly Sue stopped and started to turn back, "Wait, I have to get the bag out of the back seat."

"Don't worry, I saw it and grabbed it as you were getting out. Remember, you called me from the store, so I knew we needed the bag," Diane told her.

In a daze, Sue unlocks her door and steps into her home. She is moving in slow motion. She feels detached, just as she remembers feeling so often during her pre-teen and teen years...

Reflections

She remembers that sensation of seeing herself outside of herself when her stepfather would call her into his bedroom. Her mother would be at work, and her little sisters would conveniently be playing outside. He would have warned them not to return for at least an hour, "or else." He would not let Sue go to the neighbors to hang out because she "needed to help with the chores." He called, "Sue, come in here, we need to talk." She was excited the first time her stepfather called her into the bedroom. He had not spanked or yelled at her for two days. She had noticed him watching her, and felt very awkward, as if he was undressing her with his eyes. She was so happy he was acting a little nice to her, putting the feeling out of her mind. Despite all the times she had endured his physical and verbal abuse, she never had "left her body." However, there was that first time. She had walked slowly shyly into the room and stopped, midway between the open door and the foot of the bed, her mother's bed, his and her mother's bed. He had that smile on his face; the smile he said was just hers, nobody else's.

He patted the bed, saying, "Come here, Sue; don't be afraid."

She wanted him to notice her pretty red and yellow flowered cotton dress. She smoothed it out, and hesitated, and that was it. She took several steps toward him. He grasped both her arms, turned her around, and pushed her down on the bed. Quick as a rattlesnake, he struck her across the face, pinned her arms, and told her if she spoke to anyone about this, he would just tell her mother she had fought him. He had to discipline her. It would be as simple as that. Sue knew her mother would believe him; she always did.

He grabbed a fistful of her dress and jerked it to her chin. He thrust his rough hands into her panties, and then he tore into her. The pain shot through her body. It was at that moment she rose out of herself, up to the ceiling. She was looking down at herself, and all the pain left. She watched a part of herself disappear. Her innocence and trust shattered like one of his whiskey bottles on the tile floor.

If someone could see into the spiritual realm, one would see sparks of light leaving Sue. The blueprint matrix of her life resets as the new algorithms fill with hurt. Sue's future altered forever.

** **

Sue is startled as Diane grabs her by her arm. As if she stepped out of a motion picture from the past, back into reality. The flashback is gone as rapidly as it came.

Sue, one last time, tries to convince herself she may not be pregnant by stating aloud to herself, *we used protection and I just had my period, I didn't think we needed extra precaution.*

Diane leads her into the kitchen and pours diet soda over crushed ice in a mug. Diane fills the silence with chitchat about her day;

Sue sips her drink, feeling the cup grow slick with condensation. She nods at appropriate times, but soon disconnects, feeling only the cold, bubbling cola slide down her throat and into her turbulent stomach.

She smells the faint odor of the trash she had not taken out to the curb the night before. Her stomach begins to roll against the icy cold soda; she sloshes the sweaty mug to the table and rushes to the bathroom, banging into the doorframe on the way. The jolt to her shoulder rouses her from her stupor, and stabbing of pain overcomes the churning in her stomach. She slides on her knees and catches the rim of the toilet just in time to heave up the coke that had barely made it past her throat. It felt like acid and tasted just as horrid.

"Alright, when you're through hugging the toilet, turn around and sit so you can pee on this stick" says Diane.

Diane follows her. She hands Sue a wet yellow washcloth to wipe her face and mouth. Then she hands her the stick and leans against the sink to wait.

Sue looks up and weakly grins, "Thanks a lot." Her head is spinning, her knees shaking; she pulls up her skirt, down her panties, and takes the stick from Diane. With a warm yellow stream, she saturates the stick and passes it back to Diane. Diane is prepared and has another washcloth to hold the stick and place it in the container. Sue finishes, flushes, and joins Sue to watch the yellow circle turn purple. Sue blinks her eyes, hoping she did not just see what she has seen. She looks desperately at Diane, already prepared for the potential emotional collapse.

"Sue, it is positive," Diane whispers.

Tears trickle down Sue's face, and a moan moves to a deep wail, "No! This can't be happening..."

Inside the womb, little one is jolted and thrusts around. The saturation of sadness moves through her little form. Deep sensations of feeling unwanted surges through the tiny being and she yearns for her heavenly home that embraces her existence.

Sue's sobs begin to subside. Diane leans closer to the mirror and studies her blue, slightly Oriental eyes, and black spiky hair. She wonders if she really is a good friend after all.

Reflections

She knew Jorge was nothing but a male slut. She had known him in high school. Even then he had been charming and arrogant enough to lure any unsuspecting female five years his junior or five years his senior. Despite his name, his coloring was not too dark, and his eyes were green. He played wide receiver for the Lakers at Max S. Hayes High School. Girls drooled as he performed on the field, flashing his perfect, white grin, with sweat pouring down his face and soaking his royal blue and white jersey. He seemed to shine like some mythical, larger-than-life king, on the field, and in the hallways of the school.

What irony, a month or so ago, Sue ran into Jorge, she literally ran into him as she hurried out of a Starbucks and he rushed in. Sue managed to toss her entire Mocha Latte grande in the center of his pristine, starched white shirt. The humor on his part and the embarrassment on hers led to a swift, lust-filled romance. When she heard the details from Sue, Diane mused, there was Jorge, still loaded with charm. Turns out, he had earned a bachelor's degree in political science from Mount Union College in Alliance, Ohio. He had lived on campus then, and had played college ball, but only second string. Now he was applying for law school and working part-time at a large firm downtown as well as a local bank.

* *

Recalling those details while gazing into Sue's bathroom mirror, Diane ruminates, *Did I encourage Sue to go ahead and indulge in some delectable and decadent sex? …Sue? …the shy and serious one?*

Sue pushes Diane aside, and says, "Okay, I look like a bullfrog with as many tears as I have shed. Move, so I can wash my face and put on some more makeup."

Diane isn't sure how long she has been starring at herself, but she realizes Sue has a determined look on her face and has formulated a plan as she fixes her face.

"So, what do you have in mind," Diane asks provocatively.

Sue takes a deep breath, musters up her courage, and says, "I plan to call Jorge and ask him to have dinner with me at my apartment. I will fix something delicious, with a few beers to soften him up."

"Then what?" asks Diane.

"Then, I am going to calmly tell him I am pregnant, and that I want to keep it."

Diane has a deep, heavy feeling in her stomach that signals Sue's plan is not going to go well. She quickly readjusts her face from an obvious smirk, to a consoling look and asks, "Sue, why don't you wait awhile? There's lots of time left and sometimes babies just naturally miscarry. Maybe, if you wait, you won't have to deal with Jorge at all about it."

Sue twirls around so quickly that Diane ducks, afraid she is going to get bitch-slapped.

"What are you talking about? This is his child too, and he needs to be informed and be a part of the baby's life, even during the pregnancy. He always jokes about the cute kids he will have. So what he is only 24 years old? That is old enough to feel some responsibility as a parent. Even if he doesn't want to be with me, he will want to be a Dad. His Dad has always been involved in his life, telling him every move he is supposed to make. He knows how important fathers are." Sue feels on the verge of panicking…*this child cannot grow up fatherless like she is. He will have to be involved or she just could not bear the thought.*

The internal movement of the fetus has fluctuated extensively over the last hour. Chemicals and energy diffuse confusingly, within and without, flooding Sue's body. To the tiny Being, one moment feels diminutive, and the next cherished and valued. She is exhausted, uncertain about her belonging, and yearning for acknowledgement. She longs to hear her mommy's voice.

That night, or perhaps the wee hours of the morning, Sue lies on her back, looking up at her ceiling, watching the reflections and shadows scurry around her room. Outside her window is an old, sturdy oak tree that is full of luscious green leaves following a very cold winter. A fleeting thought crosses her mind, but more located in her heart-throat region, "What doesn't kill you, can make you stronger." She wonders who told her that, as she gazes out the window to the oak tree. Remembering how barren and dead it looked this winter, wondering if it had "bit the dust," from the cold, hard freeze that had lasted over 2 weeks.

"Another one could bite the dust," chanting in her memory, echoing words and refrain, "another one... and another one...." Curiously, Sue's thoughts shift; she slowly places her hand on her belly. She ponders; perhaps another one may bite the dust... *I have thought about abortion several times today.* She could get an abortion without telling Jorge about the pregnancy. Sadly, she thinks, *and another one would bite the dust... Another human essence, created out of stupidity and a moment of indulgent pleasure, with no thought about its potential life, potential future...* What a tragic thought.

Another jingle and refrain: "What doesn't kill you can make you stronger." These words flood in, like warm water bathing her tormented soul... Sue wonders, *Could this be about me, or about this child I am carrying. If I don't kill it, will it be stronger because it survived the odds?* She feels drowsy, and warm and cozy as she dozes off. She softly pats her tummy, and says, "Don't worry little one, we will both be stronger!" From the moment of conception, this is the first sensation "little one" has experienced where she felt energized and hopeful. She twirls around in the womb and somehow knows, no matter what happens next, she exists for a purpose.

CHAPTER 2

Jorge wakes up and immediately remembers he has to finish an extremely important paper today. The paper is part of the screening process for his acceptance into law school and requires applicants to write in 200 words or less, "the reason you wish to attend law school." Writing about his academic achievements is easy, as well as integrating extracurricular activities. Besides sports and women, Jorge couldn't really add much else. He hadn't made any meaningful contributions to society. As he yawns and stretches, Jorge asks himself, *why do I want to attend law school anyway?*

He crawls out of bed and slowly passes by the mirror in the hallway. Out of habit, he glances at himself, automatically flexing his muscles and smiling at himself. He walks into the bathroom, and runs his long fingers through his black, wavy hair. He catches a faint whiff of female as the fingers pass by his nostrils. He deliberately brings them to his nose again, one by one, and then lightly licks them to see if there is any salty residue on their tips. *I do love women*, he tells himself.

What was her name last night? The woman he met in that nightclub... He had been thinking about Sue, but a delightfully ditzy blonde-haired woman approached him, and asked if he wanted to dance. She bought him three Crown Royals and coke, unaware he already downed two before she came over to him. *Oh, yea, her name is Barb*, he remembers. She offered to take him home, but instead, they drove to her house. They teased and tantalized each other until about 3 am. He clearly remembered the time because her cat had jumped up on him and had started biting his fingers. Yuck, he forgot that cat had been nibbling on the fingers he just licked. He threw the cat off the bed and it knocked the clock over. When Jorge saw it was 3 am, he had nudged Barb and told her she needed to take him home. She was not too cordial at that hour, probably a little hung over herself, not to mention sore from the sex escapade he had provided. *Women complain in the moment, but always come back for more*, Jorge told himself. *She won't be any different from the others.*

While he switches between thinking about why he wants to go to law school, and the blurry events of the night before, he is on autopilot. As he showers, he thinks, *For sure, it is what my father expects.* Finally, as he shaves, Jorge realizes, *Father believes my going to law school will increase his social capital in politics. He thinks I'll follow his lead and be the second- generation politician.* By the time he brushes and flosses his teeth and styles his hair, he wonders who will call first, Barb or Sue. With a towel wrapped around his waist, he walks into his living room. He pulls the curtains closed because the morning sunlight has started to beat a rhythm and creak through his brain. His temples begin to throb. *Damn Crown Royal never fails to create a headache the next day.* He rummages around the cabinets in the kitchen until he finds the bottle. He pops a couple of aspirin with a splash of flat beer... an old hangover remedy he had picked up somewhere. He lays some strips of greasy bacon in a frying pan, which is another hangover remedy his father taught him. The smell makes him gag and his throat feels full of acid. Every time he eats the greasy eggs and bacon recommended by his dad for a hangover, his stomach is bloated the rest of the day. *Why do I always listen to what Dad says?*

Reflections

Long gone were the days when his father had beaten the shit out of him. *Beat the shit out of me when I fumbled a pass; beat the shit out of me when I brought home a C or D,* Jorge recalls. Some nights his father would come in drunk, wake him up, pull him out of bed, shove him into the front yard, and tell him to "go long, Jorge," for a pass. If he missed one of the shitty passes his drunken father threw, his father would come after him, swiftly and with vengeance.

To tell the truth, Jorge was not a runner by nature, but the fear of his father busting his ass, trained him to run a route and had made him an amazing receiver. He thought, *maybe someday I'll need to be more thankful for what Father taught me.* After all, being an amazing receiver had got him a full ride scholarship to Mount Union College.

**

Jorge forces himself to swallow the bacon and eggs, while he wanders around his apartment. He neither likes nor dislikes the way it looks, or the fact that it had been "done" by his mother. He has blue plates, cups, and glasses; there are white and blue striped bowls, too. He believes his mother's interior touches are her way of saying she is proud of his high school football career. College, not so much... he spent most of those four years on the bench.

His father made enough contributions to the college for him to be able to continue with his scholarship, despite being on probation numerous times. He had problems getting to practices and mandatory team meetings because he always stayed out too late the nights before. Most of his coaches liked him; he was a likeable guy despite his talent for kissing ass. He also learned, "Tell them what they want to hear," from his father. He learned at an early age to agree with his father, or else... so subservience to authority had proven very beneficial in his academics, in football, and in the face of discipline for all his infractions... or the ones discovered, anyway.

While his stomach is battling his hasty breakfast, Jorge begins working on his law school admission essay. He knows exactly what to do... *tell them what they want to hear.* No one can verify or discount what he claims as "humanitarian efforts." He contrives a compelling account of feeding the homeless every week, at least. He can almost visualize himself giving a homeless man a bottle of water and a sandwich from the nearest quick stop, along with a list of shelters and the addresses and phone numbers for assistance. Jorge claims he has been performing anonymous deeds of pure altruism for the last three years, but always secretly, so "no one would find out and give me recognition for my efforts." A tear almost wells up in his eyes. *Damn, I am good. I can almost believe it myself. Amazing how our minds can convince us of anything,* he chuckles to himself. *Who cares that I never really did any of that? Someone else certainly did, because it is an awesome idea for some worthless soul who has no life!*

16

As he is feeling smug and self-gratified, his cell phone rings. Without looking at the caller id, he answers, "Hello, welcome to Jorge's whorehouse" … lol… He loves to say that, and most people laugh, except his mother. He hears a light, nervous chuckle on the other end, "Jorge, this is Sue. I was wondering if you could come over tonight for dinner?" He feels immediately annoyed with her, although he is not sure why.

"Damn it Sue, I was in the middle of working on my presentation paper for my law school application."

She feels taken aback, "Well, I am sorry. Forget I even called" She hangs up feeling humiliated, and a little desperate.

Well, that is something new! She actually hung up on me. Jorge sees Sue as somewhat serious and reserved. He certainly does not take her as a woman with any sort of backbone. *She works for Kirby Vacuum Cleaner Company for CHRIST SAKES!* As a teenager, he could barely remember her. He ran into her a couple of times in the lunchroom and then he remembers she quit school, but never really knew why. He thought she was probably simple minded, and just a good lay.

Always up for a good challenge, Jorge thinks, *hmm, she actually hung up on me. She should call back in a few minutes and apologize. Women always do that, and of course, then they want to talk about it…blah…blah…blah.*

Reflections

Jorge believes women think he is the best listener in the world. He congratulates his father for instilling that attribute, too. His father would make him repeat word-for-word what his father said when he lectured him. If he missed a single word, he would have to write a 3-5-page paper about whatever topic his father randomly assigned. The paper had to include at least three references, be typed and double- spaced, and be error free. That particular atonement was required after he hit middle school. In elementary school, if he missed a word or mispronounced something, he would have to write 500 times, "I will listen with my ears and keep my mouth shut. Father had a way of getting his point across, both by brain and brawn, Jorge recalled.

He throws on some jeans and a "wife beater shirt." He thinks the name appropriate. His father always wore "wife beaters" after he came home from work and then that was exactly what he did. Jorge remembers his mother begging and pleading for his father to stop hitting her. He had felt so helpless. Even as a little tyke, he wanted desperately to stop his father from the onslaught. At his attempts to intervene, his father would tell little Jorge, "Every time you make me get you out of the way, I am gonna hit your mother even harder, and then you can blame yourself for these bruises."

He made sure her face looked beautiful, and carried the bruises on her arms, legs, stomach, and chest. He thinks to himself, *Father always said he didn't like her wearing tank tops anyway, because men always looked at her boobs. She was shapely, even if she was his mother. She looked good no matter what she wore.*

Jorge wonders whether she went to that fundamental church to cover up what happens at home. The church has masculine gender role beliefs and would never have questions about the "Man of the House." Father attends the more liberal and politically correct Presbyterian church that does not have such fundamental beliefs, but he loves to preach them back to his wife…and never invites her to his church.

Jorge grew up with no personal religious views, but likes the way his father's church has so many social activities, and the belief that those who are predestined to heaven will get there no matter what, and those who aren't, no matter how hard they try, they just aren't going to get there. His father believes he is one who is "predestined," as well as any children of his. Of course, his mother, she prays a lot, and Jorge knows he is a constant topic in her dialogue with God… he figures, between his parents' beliefs, he is well on his road to eternal glory. No matter what direction he takes, it is *ALL GOOD*. He chuckles, *sure that God himself made me just the way I am…*

He has been at the computer for several hours, and it is now around 3pm. He hasn't heard back from Sue. The late breakfast sits heavily on his stomach, but his appetite is building. He wonders if he missed her call. Maybe he left his phone on "mute" so he could finish his project. He checks the volume, seeing it is at full volume. He hasn't had any calls since the one from Sue. He looks at his message icon and sees the "2" on the envelope icon. He feels relieved, feeling confident Sue text him, maybe describing what she is fixing for dinner. He opens his text messages and finds one from his mother and one from Barb, the blonde, from the night before. He deletes the text from Barb; he'd had enough of her when her cat attacked him. *What does Mom have to say?* "Espero que tengas un buen día, and don't forget to come over and see me this weekend!" She always mixes in a little Spanish, just to keep Jorge mindful of his heritage.

At this point, he experiences some intensity in his gut, something between agitation and concern. He immediately interprets it as agitation, perhaps a little closer to anger, rising by seconds to rage. He picks up his half full coffee cup and throws it across the room hitting the wall, and intensely yells aloud, "Dammit, why hasn't she called me back?" *F...K her...I don't need her or want her...* In his frustration, he mindlessly hits one of his familiar porn sights. He jerks off and calms down as he wipes himself off with a washcloth. *Shit, I have to change my pants; I messed up the front of these white pants.* Oh well, it helps him when he is angry, *a good way to release tension, no sense in wasting it on some Shorty*, who doesn't call him back.

He goes to his closet and picks out some khaki shorts, and a blue polo shirt. *It is a little warm anyway.* He is still unnerved about Sue; she probably is waiting for him to call her back. After all, he was a little short with her, even rude. It was not his style to call a woman back after he had been angry with her. He remembers his father never apologized, never, unless there was some sort of gain from it.

He swore for years he wasn't going to be like his father.

What the heck; he'd give Sue a call. Give her the benefit of the doubt. She most likely tried calling and he missed it. He glances at himself, and admires his muscular frame. He lifts his shirt to tense his six-pack and looks at his girth from a side view. He grins and says to himself, *Dude; you look more cut than a month ago… must be the new protein creative muscle building drink two times a day.*

Sue has kept busy all day. Saturdays are her usual day to catch up on laundry, housework, and spending time with her dog, "Ginger." Ginger is a mid-sized, two-year-old, golden Lab. She found Ginger when she was just a puppy wandering aimlessly near the jogging trail around the lake. Sue uses the track several times a week when the weather is good. Usually she has to work out in the gym until around May, and then she enjoys jogging at the park.

Sue realizes she is hyper-focused on her Saturday chores. She recognizes she tends toward extra effort and attention to detail when she is feeling insignificant or devalued. She rationalizes, *If I disinfect my home, I will feel clean and worthwhile.* She re-fills the sink with water for mopping, and mops around the legs of her walnut kitchen table. She notices the wood pockmarked with impressions of her dog's teeth. She sighs and is grateful Ginger has passed her chewing stage.

Ginger glances at her and catches Sue's eye as her tail wags in glee. She ambles over, nudges Sue's leg with her wet nose, and waits for petting.

"What are you gonna do with a little one running around and pulling your tail and ears," Sue asks the dog.

Ginger seems to understand. She flops down on her back at Sue's feet and rolls over on her belly.

"Yeah, yeah, you think you will just surrender to a little curious and rowdy kid around here? I will believe it when I see it," Sue says, reaching to rub Ginger's tummy. She continues, as if Ginger could understand, "So much for the meal with Jorge, I should have known better anyway."

Sue feels a deep sense of rejection, but attempts to come to terms with raising this baby without the father involved. Tears well up in her eyes, and there is a deep ache in her heart, as she tries not to think about all the complications of being a single parent.

When the phone rings, Sue holds a slight hope it is Jorge. She chides herself for believing he might have actually cared about her. She lets her cell phone ring three times, as she wrings the mop, and then pushes it aside. She has to sort through the clutter on her kitchen counter to find her phone. It is still ringing in the midst of the canned goods and boxes she piled there while reorganizing her pantry.

Reflections

The compulsive organizing is a form of her rejection therapy. She has had some form of this ritual for many years. Before she lived on her own, she would clean and organize her drawers, and closets. Her lazy mother and stepfather demanded her assistance in housework. It was the only way she'd ever receive any form of praise from either of them. "Thanks, Sue, you know you do such a better job than I do in the kitchen. Sue, your sisters love you to put away their toys and make their room look so good. Sue, I just can't get the bathroom as clean as you get it…" Sue held onto the few accolades allotted from her mother's self-centered world. Of course, the consequences for not complying could range from using guilt, grounding, being left alone with the stepfather, or being raged at with horrific name-calling. It was never predictable, so cooperating appeared to be the least path of resistance, and kept her busy so her stepfather was less likely to have time alone with her.

* *

She picks up the phone but before she can say a word, she hears, "Well, it is about time you answered one of my calls."

Oh shit, she says to herself, *I forgot to look at the name.*

It is her mother. No matter how hard Sue tries to avoid her, Sue's mom always finds her. She is relentless, "Sue, I do not know what has   gotten into you? You seem to have forgotten who brought you into this world and who raised you and your sisters primarily by herself. Do you have no gratitude? You know, I never cease to be amazed at how unappreciative you are for all I did for you."

"Mother, you seem to have forgotten I have been on my own since I was barely 17, and I am doing quite well without your help."

Her mother changes her tone a little so Sue won't hang up on her. "You know Sylvia will be graduating high school next week and she really misses you. Sarah is going to be in her junior play the night before graduation, and both of them want to see you. Have you sent your sister a graduation present? You know Sarah just turned 17 last week. She wonders why she didn't get a present from you."

Her mother knows how to use her sisters to suck her back into her antics. Her mother, Samantha, or Sammie, knows how deeply she loves her sisters. She had taken care of them so much when they all lived in the same house. Although they are only 2½ and 3½ years younger than Sue is, she feels like they are her own children.

Reflections

All the time Sue cared for herself and her sisters, her mother picked loser after loser, attracting men who quickly made it plain they were more attracted to little girls than to a grown mother of three. Sue acted like the decoy, staying home while her sisters took part in any number of school activities that kept them away from the house as much as possible. Sue knew what Sylvia and Sarah would face if Sam's latest "love of my life" got them alone.

**

"Sam," said Sue, knowing that using that nickname would infuriate her mother. She really hopes her mother will just get pissed and hang up on her.

"Please don't call me Sam. I am your mother. I am going to overlook that this time, but I need to know if I can count on you to be in town to stay with your sisters for their activities."

Sue asks, "What do you mean, Mother? Are you telling me you're not going to be there for Sylvia's graduation and Sarah's play?"

"Sue, I have an opportunity to go to Canada for two weeks with Tom, and the slopes will still have some snow on them."

"Mother...who is Tom?" Sue asks warily.

"He is my new boyfriend."

Sue feels trapped and angry. She takes a deep breath and wards off the surging panic attack she feels rising with her heartbeat. She switches to "speaker," puts the phone down, and begins to wipe the shelves in the pantry. Soon, she is scrubbing so hard, the paint is coming off.

She says with sarcasm as rough as her scrubbing, "I thought you swore off men after the last one took your credit card and used it until it was maxed it out?"

Sue never believes the bullshit her mother tells her. Half the time what she says about others is really, what she is doing herself. She needed money and did her "whining victim act" until Sue gave her $50 or whatever she could afford, during that time. She'd be there for her sisters; she always had been. She concentrates on cleaning, letting her mother just ramble on-and-on.

"Come on Sue, you know your sisters think the world of you. Besides, six months ago, you told me you would be able to have a week's paid vacation by spring, and knowing you, I doubt you have taken it, yet."

Damn, Sue thinks to herself, *how charming and convincing my mother can sound.' She cringes inside, thinking how venomous she could be when she didn't get her way. If I go now, I can ward her off another six months and ca postpone having to tell her about the baby. I can just tell Sarah and Sylvia, I've got a stomach virus or something if they notice me throwing up. It's a good way to get away from Jorge and regroup anyway.*

She decides this all inside herself, and before she knows it, she's told her mother she'll ask for the week off, and let her know tomorrow about the details.

Having gotten what she wants, and knew she would get from Sue, her mother, Samantha, becomes charming and engaging, "Sue, I can always count on you."

"Mother, I will call you; please don't call me again… please…" Sue hangs up the phone with a mixed sense of dread and relief. She finishes reorganizing her cabinets and finds some satisfaction in seeing the cereals, soups, and canned goods lined up symmetrically. Then her phone rings but she flips it to silent, knowing it must be her mother again. She doesn't even look at her caller ID.

His call unanswered, Jorge, slams his phone down with an uncommon feeling of distress that Sue doesn't answer his call. He heads to the gym, intending to grab a bite to eat afterwards. *She's not going to ruin my evening*, he decides.

Sue sighs deeply after her decision to ignore the phone call she was sure was from her mother. She feels exhausted and confused. Did she actually just consent to going to stay with her two sisters next week? She tries so hard to avoid her mother and to be too busy to get sucked- in to her drama. For years, the cardinal sin has been, *never tell any plans in front of mother. Keep it general or Mother will somehow, someway catalog the information into her predatory mind to use for her own gain in the future.*

In her mind, Sue sees her mother as a predator just like the men who were in and out of her mother's life, and the lives of her and her sisters. Her mother chose men she could conform and enslave to her will. At least that is how Sue saw it as a child. Now, as an adult, and after reading numerous books about the alcoholic family, it is obvious a narcissistic mother raised her. The world revolved around Sammie and those in her world revolved around her, at least in her mind.

Reflections

Sue recalls the time when she was seven, before the sexual abuse. She was already doing most of the chores. One Saturday, she was watching her little sisters and helping them clean their room. She was anxious to be done because her mother had told her, "If you're a good girl, and you get the room cleaned, you can go roller skating with GG." Gloria Gail, or GG, was her best friend in the neighborhood. She was a cute, blonde, blue eyed china doll, and her mother always dressed her so cute. Sue fantasized that GG's family would adopt her, but feared her father would be unable to find her, or know where to look, if he came back for her. He wouldn't even know her new name.

Sue remembers working diligently to clean up her sisters' room. She was just supposed to be helping, but Sarah and Sylvia preferred agitating her instead of pitching in. It was easier and quicker to do it herself, but quite frustrating. Sylvia would go to the toy box and pull out toys as soon as Sue would get them into the box. The last time, Sylvia had completely unloaded the box and was standing in the middle of the pile of toys without a shirt on.

Sue heard the front door open, but it was her stepfather, not her mother. Sue didn't know if he and her mother were married, but he was her sister's father, or so they were all told. Mark was tall, and always wore jeans with a big buckled belt, dirty cowboy boots, and shirts that would show his hairy chest. His face was scruffy and unshaved. His hair was thin and wispy. He had deep, penetrating, dark brown eyes, with a scar over his right eye he claimed he got bull riding.

He said, "Sue, your mother called me right before I left work, and said I was to check on you and the girls. She said if I thought you done a good job, I could take you roller skating, but if I didn't, then you would have to stay home and finish your work."

He looked around and chuckled to himself, "Guess I won't have to get back out after all."

Sue began to protest and sniffle, "But, Sylvia just did that!" I have been working hard…"

Her pleading fell on deaf ears. Then, it dawned on her that her mother never intended to let her go. She wanted Sue to stay home to take the load off her! Sue's theory proved true when Sammie came home, griping, as usual, about the other women at work. She had her blue work uniform on, with her nametag and little tags that read, "Employee of the Month," "Most Outgoing." Sue couldn't remember what was written on the other little tags. Her mother asked Mark if he had thought about dinner as she continued walking into the room. She saw Sue sitting in the corner, hands over her face.

She jeered at her daughter, "Well, I thought for sure you would be skating."

Sue could tell it was insincere, but her theory proved true even more when her mother said, "Oh well, I need you to help watch the girls tonight. We are going out with some friends from work. Sharon asked me to her birthday party at the last minute, and I told her I wouldn't have a sitter. I guess your laziness has served a greater purpose. Maybe next time you can get their room finished and learn to have fun like your Mama."

* *

There in her clean, organized kitchen, Sue thinks, *once again, it is all about Mama having fun. I'll take a hard-earned week's vacation and be the surrogate mother, with no maternal rights, but only maternal responsibilities.*

Sue wonders if the cycle will ever end. How much longer will she fall prey to her mother's self-centeredness?

Sue has all but forgotten about dinner with Jorge, when suddenly she feels very hungry. She realizes she has not eaten much all afternoon. She is uncertain if she feels movement... or if it was it just her imagination. *Little One* experiences an uncomfortable sensation. A sensation she would later understand to be "hungry," but for now, she protests in uterus by flitting around in circles, hoping the feeling would find relief.

Sue grabs some whole-wheat crackers and cheese, and a glass of juice. She seems able to tolerate a snack like that without the urge to vomit. She finishes six crackers and feels better. The tiny being, also becomes content as the blood sugar level responds and her nutrients move through the placenta. She nestles to the side of the wall lining for cushioning, and falls fast asleep dreaming of her celestial home.

CHAPTER 3

Sunday is a complete blur for Sue. She has worked many weekends over the last 3 years and finally managed to work her way up the ladder into management. That means better pay and most of the time weekends are completely off, unless your team scheduler botches up the schedule for the upcoming week and then, the manager's role is to intervene and rearrange the schedules. That is what she has been doing since around 8 am Sunday morning. She wakes up to go pee at least 3 times during the night, and by 7 am she is nauseated.

She is finally getting some morning sickness relief. As described in her HEALTH magazine, if she eats some protein such as peanut butter and crackers in the middle of the night, her blood sugar would not plummet. The article indicates the drop in blood sugar causes the nausea, and intake of protein will keep it more stable through the night. She forgot to eat her crackers and peanut butter at the 3 am bathroom break, so by 7am her stomach is churning. She finds herself fumbling in her now organized cabinets, so organized, she forgot where she set the peanut butter. At the spot between the Maple syrup, and jelly, she spots it and then her phone chirps. It is in her robe pocket and she opens a text from the Senior Management leader to revise the schedule and have everyone contacted by noon.

The subordinate sales teams are primarily single and most, like Sue when she started, do not have much of an education. Unfortunately, Sue did not climb the ladder quite as quickly as some people did; mostly because she would not sleep with the Senior Management partners. One in particular, named Jack, is 10 years her senior, who presented himself as a caring mentor.

Reflections

She remembers once when he asked her to come to one of his team planning meetings to strategize some route changes. When she arrived at S & B Burgers to meet with the team, she saw Jack sitting there at the bar, by himself with two beers in front of him. As she

approached him, he greeted her with his pearly white smile, stood up, with his perfectly starched white dress shirt and brown sports coat, and hugged her a little too friendly and a little too intimately, saying, "I guess it is you and I kid…no one else could make it." Sue couldn't help staring at Jack's thinning brown hair draped to one side, covering the ever- growing bald spots. She endured the meeting, which was more of a "we need to spend more time together talk," as well as his hands landing in between her legs numerous times before the "meeting" was over. He wanted to continue at his apartment, but she convinced him she was feeling ill and needed to go home. That was one of several approaches she had endured from him.
**

Fortunately, her efficiency and organizational abilities landed her a spot on the management team, despite Jack's perpetual attempts at seducing her. Her sales team consists of Gail, Robert, Randall, and Jennifer. Gail is an eighteen-year-old female, with extremely masculine traits. She was most likely a "bull dagger," rather than a "lipstick lesbian." She isn't exactly sporty, and certainly looks more like a truck driver. She is about 5ft. 2 in. with dishwater blonde hair cut short, almost like a military cut. She doesn't have any discernible shape beneath the loose-fitting clothing she wears. It is beneficial to have her on the team. She is tough and although the team doesn't have a truck to drive to the residential locations, they do have a 4 x 4 four-wheel drive conversion van, which drives similar to a truck. Conversion vans aren't typically used commercially; however, Quigley's Motor Co. began selling vans for those with large amounts of cargo or people, of which Kirby has both.

Besides Gail commanding the sales ship van, she also is no sexual threat to Sue. Gail is a one woman's woman, and she is currently in a 2-year relationship with an older "lipstick lesbian," who rescued Gail from a life filled with rumors, ridicule and an overzealous religious mother who insisted Gail attend a private Catholic School. Miserable in her blue pleated skirt, and white pressed starch collared shirt, her girlfriend delivered her to wear blue jeans, and flannel shirts, or tee shirts, depending on the weather.

Robert is the *oldest* on the team. He is a ripe old age of 25 years old, and happily resigned himself to selling Kirby vacuum cleaners the rest of his life. He may not be the brightest lamp on the post, but he is a bright spot for working for Kirby Co. He is tall, thin, with a square jaw line, and a nice smile, despite his crooked teeth. Regardless of the despicable stories of criminals who work for Kirby, Robert is clean cut, honest as the day is long, and is consistently entertaining as he spills the latest and newest information on any new Kirby model or latest statistic related to the vacuum cleaner world.

He had been married briefly to a woman he met in the suburbs while demonstrating a vacuum cleaner, but he traveled too much for her, so she had a fling while he was out of town. He somehow managed to get over it. After a few tears, and beers and a couple of days off, he renewed his smiles, and vowed his only love to be Kirby vacuum cleaners. One day, shortly after he found out she had an affair, Sue overheard him talking with Randall, and he said, "Well, at least when the Kirby sucks so good, it don't rip your heart out afterwards..." She didn't know whether he was being sardonic or serious, so she had to turn around and go to the break room to laugh out loud. That's just how seriously funny Robert can be.

Randall is 22 years old, and an extremely serious introvert, until he puts on his sales rep. mask. He goes from a sullen, morose kind of guy, to a gregarious, animated sales machine. It almost resembles the movie "Sybil," as he changes his speech, affect, and even body posturing. As an introvert, he slumps over; his hair covers his right eye, he seldom looks directly into your eyes, and he mumbles. When he goes into his sales mode, his hair flies back, his eyes become piercing, as the blue/green color shift and change. He is loud and articulate with a sort of mesmerizing effect. Although weird, Sue is happy to have him on her team. He is one of the top sales representatives in the region, making her salary better.

Finally, there is Jennifer, a 23-year-old Hispanic female, the stabilizing force to the motley team. Jennifer is a reasonably attractive looking woman, with the traditional long black hair, dark brown, piercing eyes, full lips, and a conspicuous smile. However, more than that she is logistical and intuitive, making practical suggestions and offering encouragement to her teammates. She is consistent and accepting. She tends to be a bit of a "bible thumper," but does "practice what she preaches." Therefore, overall, Sue has felt on top of her game.... until this pregnancy...

Sue contacts Jennifer, in between visits to the throne of existence, her toilet. She is either peeing or spewing up her latest efforts at nourishment. Jennifer offers a great distraction strategy during a discombobulated week when everyone is miffed. Jenn suggests they give them the rara-hoopla and tell them "if we keep going at the rate we are going; we are sitting in first place for the Hawaii trip." Sue gets off the phone with Jenn, and is pumped up herself when she thinks, *Wow, how am I going to lead this team to their goal of a paid for trip to Hawaii next year, being pregnant?* Worse than that, will she even be able to go to Hawaii if they win the trip with a newborn? UHHH...she won't think about it now.

The womb jostles, once again the distant rumbling of feeling unwanted and undesired, the small spirit grieves inside of her....

CHAPTER 4

Over the last several days, Jorge has been preoccupied with his efforts to get into law school. Jorge determines to detach the strings as his father's puppet son. He has been resistant to answer his father's phone calls and avoid his "surprise visits." Jorge, with the help of destiny, masters the creation of a hidden pact with his father's secretary, Amy. This pact is a reluctant agreement on Amy's part, to text him every time his father indicates he will schedule a break for him to "go and check on my son." Thus far, he has avoided four confrontations to this escapade.

Now, why does his father's secretary have this allegiance to Jorge? This is a great question. Perhaps it has to do with last month, while settling into his position, upstairs in the VIP area, following a great medium rare steak at the Secret Gentleman's Club, drinking his third whiskey tonic. He is already horny after watching the floor girls. He arrives before 4pm, as admission is only $10 bucks, saving his cash for the upstairs room that is $20.00 entry and then $20.00 per song. Jorge has made an oath to himself to indulge in $100.00 nights. He is weaning off his financial dependence from his father. He is already up to $50.00 and wanted to have at least two lap dances. It usually takes him two or three songs to get his rocks off.

Therefore, there he sits, feeling ready, relaxed, and desirous of a good time. These girls most likely are not ever going to run in his social circle, since most are from the Hilltop, Bottoms, Powell or Dublin area. His head is down, eyes closed, as he listens to the rhythm of the music, in anticipation. He feels her touch, and grasps her hand as she swiveled and swayed her tight ass on his lap. He is hard already…he wants to see her face, but patiently waits. The lights are dim, and he feels surreal. Here, no performance is needed from him, unlike when he is having sex with a woman. Here, he doesn't feel like he must perform and be his best. Usually he feels whomever he is with, must want him again, so he can have her and then throw her away. Probably in a weird way, how his father has treated him.

He sits there, feeling an odd sense of surrender, when the sexy babe, slowly turns around. "Oh my God, Amy…what the hell," he exclaims with surprise and disgust… They both about come off their chair, and not the sort of coming off Jorge thought. She is so embarrassed; she almost knocks down the girl who is in a precarious pose next to her. She flees out of the room, and he is in shock…Instinctively, almost predatorily, he begins to form his plan.

Amy shyly approaches his chair fully clothed. She said, "I do this to earn a little extra income to pay off my student loans. Please, whatever you do, don't tell your father…I know he would fire me immediately!"

Jorge, being a chip off the ole' block, didn't skip a beat. "Oh, I understand, Yeah, you are right, he is very conservative in his views; although he doesn't practice his own conservatism… Hmm, I could use a favor in exchange for my secrecy." At that moment, he has a ticket he can cash in when needed, and he needs it now. He wants to do this on his own. To find value on his own… without his father's influence, prestige, power plays…

Chuckling to himself as he thinks of Amy's eternal gratitude for him not sharing her little secret, he refocuses himself on his Law School acceptance agenda. He has gone onto numerous websites to figure out what he needs to do. He has been following the five steps to get into law school:

1. Take the LSAT; 2. Register with the LSDAS; 3. Decide Where to Apply to Law School; 4. Write Your Personal Statement; 5. Get Recommendations.

He has already prepared his personal statement, number 4 of what he needs. He has it almost completed and believes the benevolence adds a nice touch, topping off his football career. His grades have not been his forerunner so he knows he must score high on the LSAT. Just yesterday, Jorge   joined a study group called lsat meetup@lsat.meetup.com/. He is online chatting for at least an hour discussing how, when and where people in his area meet. In fact, he has a   horrific headache. He is unsure if it is from the new use of his brain functions, or the residual hangover after having a few brews to congratulate himself for his new determination and efforts.

He completes number 2 and registers with the LSDAS, which is the Law School Data Assembly Service. It is supposed to be helpful in finding the right match for Law school and student. Thus far, it has not been too beneficial, since his high school and undergraduate grades were not exactly reflective of his potential, but rather his lifestyle. *Who would have ever thought being so HOT could cause such problems. It just doesn't seem right!* ...feeling a bit insecure and inadequate, he humors himself.

Jorge reflects, *I just want to be like Sean Bedford,* a first year law student, a former Georgia Tech offensive line standout who seems to be just what every former football player aspires to be. He is a two-time first team All Atlantic Coast Conference center, and athlete of the Year former Gainesville Sun Scholar. He ruminates...*Sean, honored as a football player ... admired as a law student... Wow...* He is beginning to recognize his insatiable need for approval. That emotional thought generates extreme discomfort and ego dissonance. The phone rings and is a timely distraction for him. He does not have to resort to some of his more primitive defensive behaviors.

He experiences a brief sense of anticipation, before answering his phone, it may be Sue; however, his cognizance brings to mind, it is his home phone. The only person to use the home phone, besides political polling, local fundraising or random advertising, is his mother. He glances at the Howard Miller Designer Choice Allentown, 21.5", Wall Clock. He muses at his former girlfriend, Kelly, who in desperation to keep him around bought him this clock for his new apartment. She made sure and kept the price tag on it ... $195.00. On her salary, as a bank teller, it must have put a ding in her account. He notes it is a noble gesture since he hates the girly clock his mother had bought him. It is blue and white, and reminds him of his high school glory, but represents years gone by... dependency on parents and lack of masculinity. He was glad to have it thrown it away. He told his mother he had given it away to a friend who did not have a clock.

The clock indicated 6:30 pm Sunday evening, the usual time to meet for dinner with his parents. He has been avoiding his father all week, forgetting he has promised his mother he would not miss dinner. He is already 30 minutes late. He answers, before his mother has a word out of her mouth, "Mi Mama, lo siento, No puedo parar para charlar ahora porque voy tarde."

Maria automatically forgives her son. He is her only child, and has watched him go through so much suffering, unable to intervene or stop the dynamics. He is handsome, smart, and charming. Sometimes she worries about his tendency to treat women as less than how he treats himself; however, it is no wonder, with a role model like his father. He had always been respectful to her, and that was no less than remarkable to her. She says, in a loving, maternal voice, accented with a Latino accent, "O.K., see you in a little while."

Maria is 46 years old, and realizes her life is going by before her very eyes. She is a beautiful woman, who despite the abusive dynamics, has aged gracefully. Here is her son, Jorge, a grown man contending with his own problems and it is time for her to stop and consider what is to become of her future. In her culture, a second generation Hispanic, parents from Mexico City, there is the Machismo view (strong aggressiveness, male pride, or toughness). She has been speaking with her boss, about moving up in the company. She has been working for her in a variety of roles over the past several years. Harper DeBoe, her boss is an innovative female, who is a ripe old 38 years old. In 2011, Ms. DeBoe asked Maria if she could help to organize and structure her Parties and Weddings by DeBoe. She asked Maria because she has such a knack for colors, contour, and parties. The irony of being married to John Fisher of Fisher and Lott, LLC, is all of the parties he has coerced her into throwing, has increased her skill, awareness, and self-confidence. He is a commercial litigation attorney who is deliberate, determined, and if it be known, diabolical. He always gets his way.

Maria, up until recently, has avoided much notoriety in the workplace. Primarily she did not need the income, but merely wanted to get out of the house after Jorge started Junior High and no longer really needed her. Secondarily, she did not want such day-to-day contact with anyone that may notice the bruising under her shirt collar or scarf. She has been having more and more pressure to wear the designer clothing from the shop. Although, there are some conservative styles, the latest styles over the past two years have been lower on the neckline and the trend of showing cleavage. She has been able to wear a complimentary tank top with some of the dresses, but spring is here, soon followed by summer. There are times when John grabs her arms so hard, that he leaves bruises on her. She has a mocha colored skin shading some of the bruising, but as it changes from purple to green, it is more obvious.

Reflections

During the last episode with John, after he had been out drinking with his partner Bob, he came home. She was late from work after a party supply demonstration at a local mall. Her helper had to leave early because her child was sick, so Maria ended up packing up all of the crates, and having to haul them all by herself back to the store. She was preparing the meal, and admittedly, she had stopped by the Wal-Mart superstore to pick up some premade deli items, she could throw into a bowl, hoping John wouldn't notice or wouldn't care. Sometimes he is caught-up in his own world, and he barely recognizes when she has spent hours slaving over a gourmet meal. At other times, if it is not prepared to suit him, he may throw the meal on the floor demanding something else. Sometimes he would watch, or more like examine every move, until it met his approval. She never knew his mood, thoughts, or behaviors. She felt as if she lived in the Twilight Zone.

On the other hand, John brings her flowers, tells her how he cannot live without her, and could have never made it this far in life without her. She fell in love with that John. John had been a struggling law student, who would do anything for her. The zealous man helped her to get away from the family matchmaking. Her old school father, Jesse Morelos, wanted her to marry into the Hispanic culture. A man he selected for her, such as a nice Catholic boy who would be interested in taking over his grocery store when he became too old to run it. He has no male heirs, and since Maria is his oldest, he assumed she would marry someone worthy to take over Supermercados Morelos. Maria was in her second year of school at the Ohio State University, Department of Design. Her father recognized her ability to put together his displays at his market, and therefore approved of her attendance at Ohio State University. The program, ranked highly by Design Intelligence and U.S. News and World Report, made it beneficial.

Maria met John at the coffee shop on campus. He was attending Moritz College of Law and a couple years her senior. He was studying intensely, at the same time she needed to know what time it was, so she could get back to the dorm before curfew. She had forgotten her watch, and there were no cell phones back then. The clock in the coffee shop had stopped. She tapped him on the shoulder and he casually glanced up… once their eyes met, that was it. He stood up, and his 6'2" hovered over her short 5'2" frame. She gazed upwards, and time seemed to stand still. She forgot what she needed, and it was only natural for her to sit with him and drink another cup of coffee. She was late for curfew, but it was well worth it, at least at the time. John gave her courage to face her father, and figure out ways to make her father think it was his idea to let her break away from her old school traditional culture. Now, she has the insight to understand he was merely practicing his attorney principles, but at the time, she was sure he was an angel sent from heaven. Her Catholic Faith was deep, and she believed, somehow God would answer her prayers.

Anyway, back to the night of no return. John came home, and she was unpacking some pulled pork from a box. He staggered in, breathed down her neck, and began kissing it, grabbing her shoulders tight. He smelled like his usual Crown Royal and coke… she kissed him back, but was focusing on the meal. He jerked her around, and said in a menacing, dark voice, "why is the meat coming out of a box? Did you have someone else's meat tonight, and that's why you are late?" She was about to laugh it off, and tell him just to sit down and eat, when he grabbed her by her hair, yanked her to the ground, and knocked the plate to the ground. She felt the pain in her neck as he cruelly twisted her hair tight in his fingers. Her elbow hit the counter, and her leg twisted underneath her as she tangled up in her floor length, floral silk skirt. John told her to lick up the meat off the floor and then "...lick my dick, because I know you have been licking someone else's meat tonight." He was rough and brutal...more than that...degrading and humiliating.

This was the last straw. She told herself, this would be the last time she would tolerate his battering abuse. She did not have to anymore. Jorge was grown and away from home, and she would begin a plan. She acted like she enjoyed his cock with a mouth full of pulled pork and sauce he had smeared in her mouth and all over her face.

He came in her mouth, and slung the residual leakage in her face and on her hair. He finished by asking her, "Now, who has the best meat in the world?" Like a robotic puppet, feeling herself almost outside of her body, but at this point, she had some zeal at the thought of leaving, so she replied, "I hope I remember your meat as the hardest I will ever experience." Secretly, she knew she meant, if possible, never to experience hardhearted violence again... Moreover, vowed this to herself and to the Universe.

**

The universe heard her declaration, because the next day at work, her boss took her aside, and she said, "I am not taking NO for an answer, I want you to help me launch Roar on Shore, which will need a touch of decor that is right up your alley. Besides, I know you have some dark secrets that are haunting you, and I want to give you a chance for a clean break."

Maria said, "Yes, I need a plan of action to exit, but the promotion will be my first step." I am assuming it includes a pay raise."

DeBoe gets a huge smile, and says, "Yes, and of course a greater time commitment, or should I say, an alibi of time commitment while you make your plans. Maria, you don't have to tell me the details, but I have seen the bruises, seen you wince every time you move your arm and I sense somehow now is the time to begin your strategic plan. Tell me as much or as little as you want or need to. I am here and we can do this together."

* *

Dinner, with Jorge present, is the first phase of the plan: Announcing the new job opportunity. It is timely since John is considering running for a Republican house seat and the "Roar on Shore" would be a boost to his campaign. To have his wife in on a new city-building endeavor would make him favorable in his ads. It would also hold him to higher public standards, at least through the campaign. Poor Jorge, it means more pressure on him to get into law school and "make his father proud."

She hears a knock on the door, and a stomping at the front doorway. She recognizes it is Jorge, wiping off his shoes, and taking them off before coming inside. He knows the routine his father expects, and his mother has come to expect over the years of John's high standards. "Mom, where are you? I am starving…hope you made plenty. Enough for you to give me some to take home to my bachelor pad."

Jorge enters into the kitchen, where his mother is putting the final changes on her specialty of chicken enchiladas with a delicious white cream sauce. He takes a deep breath inhaling the mixture of smells, with jalapeños, cumin, chicken, fresh onions, and tomatoes blending to make his mouth begin to water. He mindlessly sticks his finger in the guacamole and his mother instinctively slaps his hand, "Dios mio!!!"

He follows the familiar ritual of licking his finger, then saying, "Sorry mom," as he kisses her on the top of her head.

She tells him to go sit down and eat some tortilla chips with the guacamole. She chatters about her day, while he sits there uneasy wondering when his father is going to enter the room. He wonders whether he should casually stand up so he can have a head start if he needs to leave abruptly, depending on how reactive his father may be to his week of avoidance.

He vaguely hears his mother comment that she has some news she is excited to share with the two of them, but has to wait until John gets home. He finds himself drifting inward as he finally has a moment to ponder why he has not heard from Sue all week. They had been going out informally for about 3 weeks and he realized she had not tried to contact him all week after she hung up on him. Maybe she is sick or something. He puts out of his memory how he had all but told her to get lost during their last conversation. Jorge, much like his father, stuffs the reality of his own shortcomings and typically passes off the wrong behavior or attitude to some other existing person, situation, or circumstance.

Reflections

A flash of recollection enters his mind as if a file system related to Sue has just popped into his brain. He remembers one of his old school mates and party friends, Diane, running into them in the mall about 2-3 weeks ago. Sue had been helping him to pick out some shirts and ties for his law school interview. Sue and Diane seemed to react like close girlfriends do. Sue hugged Diane, and they stood close together. Sue looked proud of herself for being with Jorge, and Diane actually looked happy for her rather than giving her a caddy female look. In fact, Jorge has observed over the years that women can act like good friends, but the after conversation indicates the truth. The fact is, after the hugs, kisses and chats, Sue told him that Diane is her best friend. *That is IT!!* He has Diane's phone number in his cell phone. Maybe she knows what is going on with Sue.

**

His thoughts abruptly halt as he senses a dark presence in the room. He turns around to see his father burning a hole in his back with his stare. "I see you are not dead, maimed, or in the hospital. I thought something drastic had happened considering I called you at least three or four times a day and went by your apartment at least once a day this entire week," his father says in a seething low, menacing voice. Maria clangs some dishes around attempting to distract from John's growing angry energy. He turns to her and says, "Woman keep that noise down, I am trying to listen to your son's lame excuse."

"I am so sorry Dad, my phone has been having trouble and I have been working hard on applying to law school…You know, getting all the pre-entry stuff done. I remember you telling me how the acceptance part was so difficult, and you were right." His father softens, he has fed the ego beast, and he becomes bearable. Jorge takes a breath, and knows if he intermittently feeds his father what he wants to hear, he will be satisfied. *Wow, what a miserable way to engage in father/son activity…* it is what he knows, what he has grown up with, and what is familiar. He puts himself in autopilot and disengages emotionally from his father. His mind is on contacting Diane as soon as he gets home.

They sit down for the meal and Jorge figures it is a good time to get the monkey off his back and says to everyone and no one at the same time, "Well, it will be great to hear some good news tonight." Maria takes the cue and as she places the plates in front of everyone, she sits down beside John and smiles lovingly at him. "Yes, honey I have some great news to help your campaign." John's ears perk up and he leans forward, almost getting his white dress shirt in the salsa. "Oh yea, and what might that be?" Well, I know how much voters look at how involved new candidates are in creative community projects that will build up the revenue in the city. I have the opportunity to supervise the new Roar on Shore project and show our community involvement. It will be great publicity for your campaign, having a wife supervising the project that will hopefully bring in significant opportunities for our city," she smiles, almost believably lovingly at John. He takes the bait.

"Tell me more and how involved will you be?" They eat peaceably with dialogue at a normal volume. Jorge actually feels like he belongs to a family, at least for the short duration of this meal. That is the trouble with his family, about the time he wants to disengage, they love, are kind and considerate to each other. He finds it almost impossible to break away completely. "Son, you make your father proud of you. Keep up the good work and if you need me to pull a few strings, you know I can." Rising, with a full belly, and his father getting up to shake his hand, treating him like a man, Jorge almost feels gratitude. He leaves quickly before some fight may break out taking with him the illusion of respect and love. If only for a short while, he feels good tonight, and loved by his parents.

CHAPTER 5

Diane and Sue head over to a local pub, Great Lakes Brewery off Market Avenue, to meet one of their high school friends, Latisha; current owner of a local bakery named *It Has Risen* and has done pretty well for herself.

Reflection

Latisha had been insecure throughout school, due to being a little too round, and a little too dark for a bi-racial teen. Although very pretty in the face, she rarely flat ironed her hair, and wore clothing that did not complement her figure. That is where Sue and Diane came in the picture. They were all in the locker room, after P.E. and it was right before lunch. Sue and Diane were practicing some new makeup styles, and looking over at Latisha, they asked why she seldom wore much makeup. She explained to them her mother worked two jobs and didn't have the money or time to buy her makeup or show her how to wear it. Thus, the friendship grew, as Latisha surrendered her face, hair, and fashion to whatever trend the two wanna-be beauty artists determined to bestow on poor Latisha.

Latisha's mother, Rhonda, a natural blonde beauty, raised three children primarily by herself. Latisha's father, Jacob, a 6' 5" and 275lb. large African American, ended up doing time for some white-collar crimes, when Latisha was 10 years old. When he finally got out of prison, he had a very tough road ahead of him. He had primarily worked in corporate America. Rumor has it, he took the rap for money laundering going on in his company, and ended up with a felony. Time in the Pen did not show much mercy on his career. He finally resorted to driving trucks and was gone several months at a time. Latisha never did get the story straight as to whether her father was guilty of the crime. Although Latisha's father was intermittently involved, he was emotionally unavailable most of the time. He seemed to have changed significantly since incarceration. Despite being technically free, he remains imprisoned by his own tormented emotions. He appears distant, angry, and resentful that his wife has had to work two jobs to help pay the debt accumulated during his 5-year sentencing. He was able to make parole after 3 years.

As Latisha befriended the two girls, Sue felt akin to Latisha, both of their fathers' truck drivers, and both minorities in trouble with the law. Sometimes when Sue would stay over at Latisha's house and her father was in town, she would sit down with him and watch basketball or football. Jacob wouldn't say much, but "Your Daddy would be happy to know you are bright enough… to comprehend this game…yeah…I know he'd be proud!" Sue would feel a little churn in her belly, and a twinge of hope her Daddy just might be watching the same game someplace else, but at that exact time. She had mini moments of togetherness. Not much, but it was all she had. Those were the days she still felt hope, but over the years, and after Latisha moved away from home, the moments faded, and rarely did she dare to hope or dream of her daddy or the past.

**

Sitting at the bar with her two friends, she starts to order the usual Coors Light, when she feels a twinge in her belly. Her awareness awakens, like unspoken words, "Did you forget about me?" Oh no, she remembers she is pregnant.

As the bartender asks, "Sue, want your usual Light?" Still bewildered by her new reality, she states, "No, guess I'll have a cranberry and soda."

Diana, not wanting Sue to feel alone in this venture states, "I'll take the same."

Latisha, suddenly taken off guard by her friend's drink selection, and somewhat relieved says, "Uhh, I guess I'll take pink lemonade."

The bartender sighs, "Guess I'll miss my big tip…not much of a buzz after 3 or 4 juice drinks…"

They all sort of look at each other and chuckle with reservation. Sue leans over to Latisha, "Guess we do usually tip well when we're half lit!"

Latisha gazes over with questioning eyes, Sue quickly states, "We're seeing who can drop 5 pounds the quickest," not willing to disclose her secret at this time. Latisha's countenance drops, she tugs on her too tight black dress having trouble staying down on her thighs covered by red leggings. It is obvious she has become self-conscious regarding her somewhat disproportionate figure.

The two had helped Latisha learn how to make herself look attractive despite being a larger bodied woman, but owning a bakery did not help the cause, as she was clearly no longer fitting into the outfit they had helped her pick out 2 months ago. They had all gone shopping ahead of the season to get clothes that would work for pre-spring Ohio weather, and it was tight when Latisha selected it, but she had vowed to her friends, she was going to lose the 5 pounds she needed to lose for it to fit perfectly by springtime. How ironic, she had gained five pounds and they are talking about losing five pounds from what she perceives as their already skinny bodies. Latisha feels pretty sure she has gained weight for more reasons than eating her own baked goods, but chooses to ignore her fears and definitely not share them with her girlfriends, at least not now.

Sue, most attuned to Latisha's insecurities, says, "Hey girl, you look great! If I owned a successful bakery like yours, I would be proud to know my food was irresistible!" That is the wrong thing to say. Actually, for Latisha, there are no words to console her deep sense of imperfection. Her eye makeup begins to slowly rundown her cheek as she attempts to cover her hurt with a fake sneeze and napkin to her nose.

Diane steps in to see if she can do some damage repair. "Love your shoes, I don't remember those. Did we help pick those out?"

Latisha sits up straighter, sniffles, and then takes the bait! "No, I picked these pumps out by myself and wondered if you would notice. Do you really like them? I was unsure if they looked funny with these leggings?"

Sue, aware of the successful efforts of distraction chimes in, "Love those shoes girl, wow, I wish I would have seen those first. I would love a pair just like them."

Tenderhearted Latisha, "Sue, we wear the same size, a size 8. I know my foot is a little wider, but I have only worn them once, if you really like them, you can have them before I stretch them out with my fat foot."

"No such thought," Sue says resistant and determined, as she knows how much her friend will give the shirt off her back to anyone. "They were made for you."

The mood shifts and the crisis of Latisha's self-loathing passes, when Diane's phone begins to chime an unfamiliar tone. She looks at the girls apologetically. "I know we have our cell phone off rule, and I broke it." She is about to turn the phone on vibrate, when she glances at the caller id, and sees, MALE WHORE. She freezes, and under her breath sighs, "Oh no..." Keenly aware, without a second thought, Sue grabs Diane's phone. Typically, that is no issue, but this time is different, and Diane resists Sue's gesture, holding tightly to the phone.

It rings again, and she brings it to her ear. "Hello, this is Diane, can I help you?" Sue relaxes assuming it is a call regarding a follow up appointment Diane has been expecting. However, on the other end, a deep and sexy voice addresses Diane, astounding her just by the mere energy.

"Hey Diane, how are you doing, hot thing?"

Insulted and intrigued at the same time, not wanting Sue to know who is on the other end, she sits up and speaks in her business voice, "I am well, how about yourself, how can I help you?"

"Wow, that sounds strangely sexy in a business sort of way," Jorge toys with Diane, knowing she had always given him mixed signals. One, 'I want and desire you,' and two, 'You are dangerous trouble and I better stay away!' So, despite attempting to find Sue, he thought it would be good fun to play with Diane a little bit in the interim.

"Umm, well, thank you, I think? What do you need?"

"Well darling, in all actuality, I was reminded this morning when picking out my shirt and tie, about running into you at the mall."

Diane is in shock. *He remembers me? What am I going to do if he asks me out, and Sue is pregnant with his child?* She is ruminating and within microseconds, he clears up her fearful racing thoughts. "And I remember you hugging and talking to the girl I was with, Sue," he states with a sort of question at the end. Diane is disappointed and relieved at the same time. "Yes, I know what you are talking about," still trying to keep the conversation benign from her end.

"I haven't been able to reach her, and I was wondering if you could tell me how to reach her," says Jorge.

Quickly Diane makes an impulsive, executive decision with limited contemplation on the aftermath, "Well, just so happens I am sitting right here with her."

Sue half listening since she is the team manager, quickly gears up in a business posture to manage a customer complaint or team question, "Hello, this is Sue, Kirby vacuum team manager, how can I help you?"

Laughing, Jorge says, "Well baby, I would like to set an appointment to demonstrate how well your machines suck! If I remember correctly, you have an amazing machine."

Dumbfounded, she is unclear of who she is speaking to and says with stern conviction, "Sir, I beg your pardon, but I will have to report this sort of conversation that may result in a termination of your warranty contract…or some sort of ramification. Now if you will excuse me, I am hanging up…"

"Hey, Sue, this is Jorge… chill baby, I was just joking…Well, not really about wanting another demonstration, but you know what I mean?"

Taken aback, Sue is at a loss for words. *How did he find her? How did he know she would be sitting here with Diane? More than that, what was he doing with Diane's number?* All of the questions reel through her mind as her mental processors act as if they are on vacation. "Uhh, hello Jorge, how are you doing?" She stumbles for words to say as her mental acuity feels like Jell-O jiggling on a tray.

"Baby, I have been calling and calling and you haven't responded," he lies. Of course, in Jorge's mind, it isn't a lie. The fact is, he called more than once and waited and assumed she would eventually call him.

"Sorry, I don't recall seeing your phone number or receiving any message from you," states Sue, indignant feelings rise up to take over her lack of words. The recollection of their last conversation comes flooding into her mind as she recalls she had been expecting to ask him over for dinner and he was very rude and abrupt with her. So, she hung up on him…Yes, that is exactly what happened! Her courage and temper surface pushing her to her feet. Her free hand immediately and instinctively land on her hip; a gesture imprinted in her mind. Perhaps genetic, perhaps learned, but this stance is one her mother took when determined to win an argument or reiterate her definitive point of view. There is very little Sue acknowledges that she acquired from her mother on a conscious level. However, meaning formation is not subject to one's choice, but is from experiential imprinting, as well as ancestral programming. Little did Sue know, not only did she have the maternal role model, but also inside she bore the courage of a great Seminole princess?

"If you recollect our last conversation, I called you while apparently in the middle of something important related to your law school application process… I was a disturbing inconvenience… and if you can excuse me, you are now interrupting my food order, and I happen to be extremely hungry," Sue almost yells, as she hands the phone to Diane before Jorge has an opportunity to rebuttal and defends his cause. She has a little guilt when she sees a flash of Jorge's number in her phone, but only once, and that does not count for calling and calling.

Diane stares at her friend, in disbelief she would speak to Jorge that way! *That gorgeous hunk of a male…the father of her baby and she blew him off, like lint on a sports coat.* A new surge of respect rises up in her for Sue.

Jorge is on the other end of the phone yelling, "Sue, don't hang up, I am sorry, hey really… Sue…" Diane gets back on line as she observes Sue, with everyone in the room staring at her, casually sit back down, and pick up her menu as if nothing just happened.

"Hello, Jorge, this is Diane." "No, I don't think Sue is going to talk to you," ahhh… Yes, I will tell her to call you and that you are really sorry." Diane hangs up the phone and sits beside Sue waiting for conversation.

It becomes extremely awkward, until Sue says, "I think I want this herb salad with chicken and feta cheese and sweet potato fries." That was a sure indicator the topic of Jorge is capped-off, at least for now. Latisha was preoccupied with playing Words with Friends, with some random opponent, as well as reviewing the new menu items. She was oblivious to the surrounding dynamics. She had two older brothers who fought all the time, and was skilled at "tuning out" any ruckus.

Quietly and mindlessly, the three sit there with vague female chatter about nothing and everything, at the same time. Sue, detached and disconnected, is not about to allow Jorge to reemerge into her world. She has enough to contend with pending the emerging trip to play surrogate mother with her sisters, once again. Diane, meanwhile, fantasizes what Jorge may look like right now, with muscles bulging and tension rising. She figures other areas most likely bulge at the same time. Of course, it is merely a fleeting imagination; she would never act on it. Besides, Jorge had never really been interested, or had he? Guilt begins to surface. Diane sees the image of her cheating mother, and she feels disgust towards herself. She instinctively leans over to Sue, hugs her and whispers, "I am with you, whatever you decide."

Sue breathes a sigh of relief, and thinks, *how great I have such a great friend…I am glad Diane gets me.*

CHAPTER 6

Perplexed, *once again, she hung up on me!* He feels humored by this unusual occurrence, while anger begins to surface. Aware of the inward storm brewing, he takes a few deep breaths, speaking to himself, *what did coach teach you? What did you learn from father?*

His father, John, did not allow Jorge to refer to him as Dad most of the time. He said, "If those gay priests can be referred to as Father and are highly revered, surely I deserve such respect." He reflected on being taught to use his energy for the line of attack, whether it is the football game or a life game stratagem... *when a game outcome is at stake...focus!*

He slows his breathing, deliberate, determined, and focusing on a black bird in his window. He is unaware the very presence of this bird is about alchemy and his choice at transcendence. Will his knowledge enhance the light or dark side of his existence? What is it he really wants? He is unsure if his drive to law school is by his own desires, or his father's desire for him to be just like him. His mind goes back to Sue. What is it about her that gnaws at his very core? Initially he hates feeling shoved aside. Yes, that is what he feels...shoved aside... as his father always does to him when he doesn't conform. Somehow, inside he knows it is different with Sue, but the need for conquest outweighs his introspection. He begins to contrive a plan, a deviant plan to use Sue's friend Diane to get to her. At that moment, the blackbird looks directly in his eyes. Almost with a look of disgust, he pecks the window once, appears to shake his head, and takes flight. Jorge gets a strange feeling and says aloud, "Get outta here you dumb bird. What do you know anyway?"

Diane is on her way home following the unusual turn of events at the pub. She finally talks herself into believing she is the best friend in the world, and Sue should be glad to have her as a friend that supports her advances in the workplace, as well as social life. She feels a little sad knowing Sue's world is turning around, in fact, turned around even today. She recounts Sue having to excuse herself to the bathroom after eating the wonderful lunch. She came back looking green once again, and Diane knew that lunch had gone down the toilet. What is going to happen? Sue did tell her she would be making a trip for a few days to visit her younger sisters, but said she did not plan to tell them anything because she didn't want it to get back to *mommy dearest*, as Sue refers to her. She feels it is unfair for Jorge not to know he has a baby brewing in that belly. She has a fleeting thought... *perhaps Jorge is fair game? It does appear Sue has made up her mind to detach from him.*

As if providence is reading her betraying thoughts, it selects to test her fidelity in friendship that very moment. As she is unlocking her apartment door, her phone rings again with a somehow familiar tone. Where did she hear that tone? *Oh, yes, today at the pub. What on earth, is it the MALE WHORE calling again? What does he want? She can give him Sue's number and that will be that.* Annoyed at the entire irony of the situation, she answers curtly, "What do you need now Jorge? Can't you get a hint Sue doesn't want to hear from you."

"Well hello to you, you sexy thing, I bet you know where and how to use that attitude," Jorge offers a statement question.

"Well, that depends on who and when," Diane retorts.

"I have been sitting here feeling really rejected by Sue, and I am unsure why. Since you, Diane, are her best friend, I thought perhaps I might come over and you could help me understand why." Jorge toys with Diane.

Confused and conflicted, Diane invites him over before she knows better. Exactly what is Jorge hoping for...exactly a strategy he learned from his father and perfected in his own running game? *Fake 'em out, and confuse them about the direction you are going.* What direction is he going for? He wants Diane to want him so bad; she will tell him every dirty thing about Sue, making Sue vulnerable to his knowledge. This is a wonderful combination of emotional power that leaves people feeling helpless, naked and at your mercy. It is a strong covert form of power and control.

Reflections

Jorge learned this at an early age when his father rewarded him with inviting his two best friends over, Mark and Ben. He was 8 years old the first time it happened. He recounts feeling so excited to have his first sleep over. In fact, his grades had not been very good. He complained to his father that he did not want to be in football. He said he didn't like getting tackled and all dirty. His father, oddly enough, did not yell, beat or scold him, but instead told him he thought having friends over would help him to get his priorities straight, whatever that might mean to an 8-year-old.

His friends came over, and he ordered pizza, and came in with all of them and said he wanted to tell a story to the kids. He proceeded to tell the boys about a boy he knew when he grew up who was so scared he would pee in his pants during football practice. The kids began to laugh, and then he said the little boy was a sissy and didn't like getting dirty and was afraid to be tackled. The kids asked him what happened to the little boy. He wasn't finished with the humiliation. He went on to say the boy was also dumb and failed school. With a sad face, he said the boy grew up to be a bum, and was a janitor at a KinderCare, because he was always a baby. They roared and rolled around when he said KinderCare and the man was always a baby.

His father's tactics executed with precision right into the heart of an innocent little boy just wanting to please the insatiable ego needs of his ruthless father. The next day Jorge went in and told his dad he did not want to grow up and be a janitor and wanted to be an attorney just like him. It wasn't until he was older, he began to recognize these strategies, and argue with his father. Ultimately, that is when the physical violence increased. If he would have only acted oblivious to his father's antics, he may not have endured so much pain and agony. He did learn from the best, so he was up to the challenge of getting Sue into his arms, even if it meant his clutches. One thing he learned is to never give up or give in. Where there is a will there is a way.

**

Diane feels awkward. *What have I gotten myself into…I will not disclose Sue is pregnant. That is Sue's choice.* She feels butterflies in her stomach. She goes to her closet and selects a sexy, green satin, low cut shirt and tight straight leg jeans. She throws on her cute sandals that show off her freshly painted toenails, and attractive feet. All men love her feet. She brushes her spiked hair and caresses her neck downward. She freshens up her eye shadow with a shimmery green with golden highlights, darkens her eyeliner, and thickens her already luscious lashes as she catches her thoughts and scolds herself for the emergence of her seductress coming out. How can she think like this, but then, all is fair in love and war. The beauty, the temptress is surfacing, taking over, tucking away her moral conscious. She ruminates with a growing urgency and pelvic congestion is groaning desire, *how long has it been since I've been laid? …At least 6 months!*

Reflections

She swore off men after her last boyfriend moved in and lived off her meager income for 3 months. Not only did he rarely work, but also he managed to have a never-ending supply of pot that kept him with the munchies. He was an idealist, and a freelance writer for some of the urban papers found mostly in coffee shops. He wrote articles about local artists and musicians, occasionally landing interviews and making a little here and there for his pieces. Unfortunately, she never saw his residual income as most of it went to his pot and food habit. He was ruggedly handsome, with long hair, a beard, lanky and lean. He could, on occasion pull an all-nighter in bed, but when she came in after work, and he had another woman in her apartment smoking pot with him, he had gone too far. He said he wanted to try some of the swinger's lifestyle and was interviewing her to see if they may hook up with her. That was it. She walked into the bedroom, cleared out his clothes in about 5 seconds flat and escorted, the both of them out the front door and told him not to bother calling.

She muses to herself, she is beyond that sort of thing, but her mother and father have been involved in the swinger's world, and it had ruined the relationship she had with her first serious boyfriend, Steven. They had dated a couple of years into high school and their parents began to communicate about their blossoming relationship. They were concerned about it becoming too serious too soon. She remembers one night; his parents' car parked in the driveway at her house. They were coming home from the movies and came in the backdoor hoping to sneak upstairs so they could mess around in her room. The lights were out in the living room except for some candles.

They heard some odd noises, like groans and pain, and could smell heavy alcohol. Afraid something terrible had happened, she flipped on the light, and there they all four were naked, posed in some odd pretzel positions, with various parts in various orifices. Yuck, it was more than her young mind could handle. It was more than any teenage relationship could sustain. His parents stumbled apart from her parents and made some beyond lame excuse of testing out the new carpet for skin allergens, or several other bullshit attempts to cover what was more than obvious, and disgusting.

However, there remains an elephant in the house, never mentioned. The elephant visited the fragile teen love and dumped a big pile of shit right in the middle of that romance. They could not even look at each other at school. The unfortunate thing is the foursome apparently continued their rendezvous, but would execute the ever- growing swing parties in various hotels around town. By the time Diane was of age, she moved out promptly as she was embarrassed when she introduced herself to parents, and a glimmer would shine in their eyes as they may say, "Oh, I have met your parents, what lovely people!" Diane would find herself looking the parents, considering what sort of sex partner they may be for her parents. It is amazing how a traumatic event such as walking in on parents holding another's body parts will sear into   the mind of a young

54

person. Thus, Diane continuously has some sort of ambivalence with her own sexuality. Trying to make sense of it, and attempting to conclude what is reasonable and what is not. She is reasonably sure Jorge has heard the rumors of her parents, but has never mentioned it. The invisible elephant is ever lurking around. Someday, maybe, she can move somewhere far away. At least now, she is on the other side of town.

* *

Diane decides it would be soothing to put on some soft jazz and a dish of fresh fruit and cheese. She is still full from her meal, but perhaps Jorge will be hungry. The phone rings and she absentmindedly answers with, "ready and waiting for you..."

Sue, confused, says, "Did I say I would come over later?"

"I was in such shock from Jorge's call; I forget what I did or did not say?"

"Uhh, no... My neighbor is coming over to borrow some sugar and I have it waiting for her."

Sue laughs, "Oh if she is making cookies, I am game. I am starving for something sweet after losing all of my lunch earlier. Is Hailey making cookies, and can I come over? I really could use your ear to talk things out." Diane feels the sweat beading up around her neck and under her armpits. She is agitated about the sweat, knowing Jorge will be over soon, but more than that, she realizes she is about to tell her first lie to her best friend. The temptress rationalizes it is for Sue's own good. She will help her to get rid of Jorge, which is obviously, what she wants. Before she can lie, Sue rambles, "I am just unsure what I feel for Jorge, I mean part of me wants him to just get out of the lives of me and the baby, and the other part really wants him to know, and wants to give him a chance."

Diane uses this opportunity to assist her friend in a more formative decision.

"You know Sue, he is a player, and it is not his style to settle down with one person." I have his number in my phone as MALE WHORE," Diane states with attempted persuasion.

"Yeah, I was wondering, how did you end up with him having your number and vice versa?" questioned Sue.

Happy to have a conversation diversion, Diane answers, "Oh, last year, we were at a party, and he was tipsy, and flirting with everyone. I had already heard from some of the loose women how hot he is in bed. So, one of the guys had a bet with him how many phone numbers he could get in his phone and call within the next 10 minutes. He went around the room and got as many calls as possible, and the bet landed him a bottle of Crown Royal. When he called my phone, I put his contact name as MALE WHORE."

"Oh, I guess that information helps me to stay far away from him. With my luck, he would meet my mother and she would seduce him," Sue says half-jokingly.

Diane follows up with, "Yeah, I wouldn't be surprised if he has already met my mother and father and had a double conquest."

"Diane, that is sick, really?"

"No, they only go for those who are over 40, so he wouldn't meet their strict standards."

Sue says, "It is really sad to not trust people who you want to love and respect."

Another twinge of guilt and shame flood Diane, as she hears the door. "Sorry Sue... gotta go... it's probably Hailey. We are going to go out later. Wish you called earlier. Love ya!"

"Bye," Sue hangs up, getting a knot in her gut, wondering if it is the baby, hunger, or some unknown instinct she has yet to master.

CHAPTER 7

Sue wakes up around 3am with several disturbing dreams in a row. They seem to be a never-ending intermittent sequel. She sees the Indian female running, black hair waving as the shadow of wings, her leather fringe on the beaded dress rustle through the darkness and blends with the whisper of the wind howling in the distance. It is damp and swampy, with a deep eeriness that is frightening. The troops invading the lands; a gator's silent stealth and speed. It out-maneuvers the bulkily dressed Spanish Soldier as it grasps the soldier's ankle with his menacing jaws, dragging him effortlessly, despite his anguished cry, back to his den to be dinner for its carnivorous family.

Yahola Elizabeth slips through her familiar Florida swampland. Even with her enchanting beauty and the fact, she is a Princess, these years require her archery expertise to defend her tribe. Her ancestral lineage is at stake; she reassures herself as she lightly touches the fire-hardened cane arrows able to penetrate the intricately detailed armor of the Spaniard. The Spaniards are terrified of this swampland territory and running scared. Their dry land strategies are no match for these haunted marshy lands.

She sees two of them, sitting by a dying fire, trying desperately to keep it ignited with the wet gooey wood pieces pulled out of the Cyprus trees, along with wet residual moss. She gives her howl, and out of the shadows, her brother silently slits the throat of one as the other bends over stoking the fire. He abruptly rises and she pulls out her arrow as it whirls landing straight in the center of his heart, slicing through the armor with precision. They nod and move slowly back into the shadows. Feeling satisfied, while some sense of sadness lingers regarding the uselessness of taking the life of another human being. The thought and emotion barely forming as a hand slips around her mouth and pain surges in her arm as she twisted closely to a hard metal. She twists and claws, but a blow on the head follows and she twirls into oblivion. Sue wakes up, startled, breathless, with feelings of pain in her arms, and a terrible headache.

Reflections

Who is this woman and how did she hear her name this time, *Yahola Elizabeth?* This isn't the first time she has seen her in her dreams. She saw her as a child, after her father left. She would have dreams of her flying on the wings of a wolf, with sadness deep in her dark forlorn eyes. She thought she must be some character from an old Western movie she had watched as a child. Now, she wasn't so sure. She saw her the night she found out she was pregnant. That time, she appeared shadowy; fading in and out, with a baby nestled to her breast. She just assumed it was some sort of cosmic aberration to calm her fears about being pregnant.

However, come to think of it, she appeared following her contemplation of abortion. She remembers waking up the following morning with a confident resolve to have the baby. There does seem to be some message this dream is giving to her. What is the message? She should go and kill her two no good stepfathers? LOL...this is a useless thought. Probably just because she was about to embark on a trip to see her two sisters and their presence inevitably has connections with the suffering from their worthless father.

**

She has trouble going back to sleep and as her feet hit the floor, she feels the wet nose of her faithful friend, Ginger, coming to greet her, no matter what hour. Ginger whines a little, wags her tail and heads for the kitchen, as if to say, "Come on, get up, and shake it off." Sue groggily gets up and makes herself some coffee; she slips her feet into her fuzzy house shoes, as the wooden floor caused a chill to go right up her spine. The soft lamp by the sofa illuminates just enough to create soft shadows that dance before her eyes. She sits there a while, listening to the crickets chirping outside, and a car passing every so often on the interstate several miles away. Ginger jumps onto the couch, and Sue is too tired and perplexed to object. She mindlessly pets Ginger between her ears, and pats her up and down her back. Coffee warm and steamy flows into her stomach, but it doesn't taste good this morning, and the comfort quickly transforms into nausea. Jumping up, she makes her way quickly to the bathroom with only a slight amount of acidic liquid releasing itself to remind her of her current state, PREGNANT...

Ugh, how can she forget? She has read online that coffee is not very good to drink when pregnant, and that is becoming obvious. She further realizes she needs to eat her middle of the night protein snack to help with the nausea. Her life no longer can be self-serving, but she has another human being to consider. The cheese and crackers go down smoothly and she pours out the coffee in exchange for herbal tea. Much better, or was it better? Perhaps a more accurate definition is different. Yes, life will be forever different.

Her mind goes back to the haunting dream. What about the Indian woman in her dream, what happens to her? Why should she care, after all, it is only a dream...? Or is it? She distracts herself as she checks her suitcase for all she needs to have for the week with her sisters. She glances out the window and wonders if that is the man in the moon, she sees. He seems to be smiling at her. . She rubs her tummy. Little one is aroused and swirls around happily content this night she was acknowledged. She is significant, and besides, the crackers and cheese satisfies her. She experiences sensations of gratitude and Source shines a new spark of light in little one.

CHAPTER 8

Joseph Starks sits wearily over the stacks of paperwork in front of him. It is the middle of the night and he had another restless night. He continues to have dreams, disturbing dreams. He went to see his doctor last week; however, the prescription of Ambien ended up in the trash as soon as his physician friend, Jeff Jorgenson, gave him two weeks of samples. He was reluctant to throw it away since Jeff was his long-term friend since elementary school, but felt it was better in the trash than having its seducing effects on some unsuspecting victim. He attempted Ambien several years ago, and one of his roommates said he was wandering around the front yard in the middle of the night picking up rocks and sticks randomly. When awakened, he had no recollection, rhyme or reason for his behaviors. He threw it away after that, and he would not re-subject himself to some bizarre behaviors. He chuckles as he comes to terms with the fact he never listened to Jeff anyway. Why does he go see him if he isn't going to take his advice? It is most likely the fact he found Jeff on face book a couple of years ago and they rekindled their friendship of old.

Reflections

Although Jeff is a doctor, he has gone through a terrible divorce that almost bankrupted him. He needs an objective, non-judgmental friend from his past to help put his life back together. Jeff lives in Norfolk Virginia, a nice community close to the water. Joseph misses living by the water after leaving Cleveland. He has been on the road, ever traveling and has accumulated a good amount of cash as well as learning the ins and outs of the trucking industry over the last 15 years. Jeff told Joseph he had a big house, much too large to live alone in. He and his ex-wife, Kate, had planned to have children, but medical school, residency, and starting a practice had taken most of his time. He promised Kate he would slow down long enough to have a family one too many times. She finally left him for a banker in the community who was a little younger and quite willing to start a family. She felt justified in taking all she could. She felt Jeff owed his career success to the sacrifices she made as a wife.

By the second year following the divorce, Kate is working on her third pregnancy. She left Jeff with the house stating it carried too many wasted wishes, hopes, and dreams. Besides, the Banker comes from old money, and owns the passed-down family dwelling, large enough to house children and household staff. Jeff is miserable and full of regret. Joseph has regrets of his own, so he can relate.

After researching the area, he located a trucking company for sale. He bought it at a steal, and paid cash. His amiable personality and hard work enabled him to maintain trucking acquaintances all over the North East. It didn't take more than 6 months to turn a small profit. A year into it, he was pondering the notion of buying a place of his own, but knew Jeff depended on his companionship. Jeff had dated a few women, but continues to remain primarily married to his practice. The new affordable health care act; although, allowing the masses to acquire health care, costs the private practitioners many hours with the increase caseload. His mortgage loan itself is ungodly, and Joseph contributes financial as well as emotional relief.

**

Joseph pushes his fingertips through his long black, wavy hair. He keeps himself in shape and despite being 42 years old; he looks and feels much younger. That is, except his taunting memories making him feel ancient, a man with multiple lives. He shakes his head like a dog shaking off the rain after a storm. He will not think about it; he cannot think about it. Something in the dream is pulling and tugging his memories. It seems relentless and nagging. He sees her again in his restless state. She is in front of his truck and he swerves to keep from hitting her. She causes his truck to turn around in the dream. He is headed towards the port on a foggy night and can't see. He wakes up bewildered. He ends up staying up the rest of the night doing paperwork and looking out at the moon, sensing someone somewhere is looking out at that same moon.

CHAPTER 9

She opens the door, and casually steps aside, with pouty lips and lusty heart, Diane is ripe and ready. Jorge can feel the heat as he enters the apartment. He is mildly agitated. He has looked forward to the gaming resistance of Diane and her struggle with allegiance of her friendship. Well it appears he will have no need to loosen her attachments. At this point, he will only have to focus on loosening those tight skinny jeans over that round ass. No, he tells himself she will have to play his game despite her being such easy bait. The temptress recognizes his shifting in his eyes and she knows the game is on. She immediately pulls back and walks inside. "Hey Jorge, I was about to give up on you. I have a few errands I gotta take care of. Make this quick," she lies.

He is keen and sees the fruit platter and wine glasses on the table. O.K., he knows she is gaming with him. This is good… this he likes. He can play it out. He will eventually get his way… maybe not today, but soon. "Oh, no problems, I only have a few minutes. Really, I am just here to apologize," he says believably.

"Apologize for what," states Diane.

"Oh, I realize I was putting you and your friendship in a compromising situation, and that was overly arrogant of me. Look Diane, I know we have intermittently felt things for each other, but I would never get involved with you since you are a friend of Sue's. In fact, it probably makes our relationship safer than ever. I respect you, and despite the rumors of you and your family, I notice you are discreet about your relationships. I admire that, so that is all I have to say. I'll figure all this out on my own." Jorge finishes his sentence as he is backing out the doorway and turning away, he leaves. Diane stands there speechless, her temptress scolding her for not being more sexually advancing, while her moral self is praising her for nobly maintaining friendship loyalties.

Her groins ache and she goes inside, pulling out her shoebox with her friendly pink dildo. She relieves herself, feeling humiliated sitting and eating some of the fruit and cheese she set out, then guzzling a couple glasses of wine to chase the tears streaming down her face. She hates feeling this way. What is it she really wants anyway? That sounds dumb, even to her moral self. Today, she wants to feel a warm, wet, hard body thrusting and pushing away every other thought, instead she has to resort to a cold, hard inflexible, non-entity to relieve her sexual stress. Is this what life has come to for her?

The phone rings. Maybe he is changing his mind. She answers the phone quickly. "Hey, honey this is your mom, we haven't heard from you in a while. She says, "We miss you and would like you to go out to eat with us. We are having another couple with us, but still, we will be in your area of town. So, what do you think?" Her mother asks with enthusiasm. "What the hell, why not," Diane says, with the underlying thought, "I am my mother's child!"

Jorge feels unusually unstable about his decision to leave. Damn it, he wants to get some information on Sue. He actually thinks he may feel something different for her, but wasn't he about to bone her best friend? He didn't though, and that matters to him. He has an urge to swing by and talk with his mother. She knows him better than she knows anyone. She always sees the good side of Jorge, and consistently reminds him he does not have to be like his father. He pulls into his parents' drive, willing to leave if his father is there. He isn't home and a sense of relief pours over Jorge. As he just walks in, he notices some things pulled out of the hall closet and several boxes taped with new strapping tape. One says, "TO TAKE." He wonders what that means and sits down at the piano to play a few songs while he ponders the fact it is not Christmas, Easter, Thanksgiving, or any other holiday that boxes are removed from the attic...

His mother walks quickly into the living room with a guilty look on her face. "Hello Jorge, I wasn't expecting anyone home. Your father is out of town and I rarely see you; what do you need?" She states with some resistance.

"Mom, what is going on? What are those boxes that say 'TO TAKE'?" He asks.

She starts to lie, and then she realizes she really needs her son's advocacy if she is going to pull this off. "I am going to leave your father, but he doesn't know... he mustn't know. You know he could hurt me," she pleads with tearfulness.

"O.K. Mom, jeez, calm down. You have said you were gonna leave that son of a bitch for years. What makes this time different?" He pursues answers.

"I know I have, and I have tried several times, but it is like he has a sixth sense, and he picks up on my plans, always threatening me about the things he could do to me. He used to threaten me with harming you, worse than he would already do. Then, you became the apple of his eye when you decided to apply for law school. Now, he mostly threatens me with harming my father. Things like, "I know you love your old man, and it would be a shame for him to be penniless at his age. You know I know many people who could visit his store, accidentally fall down and face an injury. Perhaps file a law suit that could last for years!"

"But mom, what could you do if he takes it out on Grandpa"? Jorge asked sounding like a little boy.

"Honey, your father is currently so preoccupied with the campaign; he wouldn't do anything to anyone that may jeopardize his career. I wouldn't put it past him feeling like he can't live without me, and threatening me, but I think I am safe right now, until the campaign is over. Just pray, he wins, and that would keep him under some constraints.

She sits down with Jorge at the piano and they play a duet of "Amazing Grace." Jorge instinctively wraps his arms around his mother and hugs her deeply. "I understand Mom... can you tell me your plan? You know I get so scared of receiving a call that you have mysteriously disappeared and I would be relieved to know what you are doing instead of wondering," he feels a little desperate.

"Son, I am not going to place you in a compromising situation of knowing the details, but if and when your father asks where I am, tell him I had to go to the old country to see mi tía. Say I will be gone for at least two weeks. She lives rurally in Mexico and he could not find her house if he tried. I have been telling him she is sick and I am worried about her. I will be in touch with you. I have bought a phone for you and I to communicate. Keep it in the trunk of your car. Now, what is bothering you, mi niño"? She instinctively asks.

He has a lot to take in, and the thought of his mother fleeing to Mexico makes him feel even more alone in this world. He remembers Sue, and his newly found feelings of drive and desire. Perhaps it is a procreative instinct, something primitive in humanity to settle down, procreate, and multiply. Isn't that what his father has done? Does he really love any of them, or is it about him multiplying himself on the earth? He even admits to his mother womanizing and being rude and arrogant with Sue.

She sighs, "Ahh, Mijo, you sound so much like your father. You must find a better way, a reason to live besides just being so powerful. It takes more of a man to surrender than to exert power. Go to the chapel, kneel at the altar and pray. Ask God to help you overcome these demons in you. Perhaps there is some solace for your soul and you will find your answers. We all have to find our journey. The key is, is our life road a pathway of love, hope, peace, kindness, and faith, or hate, anger, power, fear, and control? This is between each person and his or her Creator.

I have tried to honor my vows and be committed to marriage; however, there comes a time when each person's value needs expression. I am important, talented, and valuable, and I am not going to accept abuse as a worthless piece of nothingness. That is just not true and God has given me courage, faith, and hope to live out the rest of my life in peace and safety." She slowly walks over to her purse and pulls out a small, simple, pay by minutes go phone, and hands it to Jorge. "None of us deserve to live each day like walking on eggshells," she finishes with a sigh.

He remembers feeling that feeling around his father, but worse than that, he hears in his mind, some of his last several girlfriends making that exact statement. They all said the same thing, "Jorge, it feels like I walk on eggshells around you." It would be shortly after that he would break up with them. Maybe they were only reiterating how much he was like his father, no matter how much he protested. He feels emotionally drained and helpless, like the many times he had his father yelling, scolding, and hitting him. Nothing matters; nothing can stop the hollow feeling inside. His mother lovingly caresses his cheeks, and she rises up telling him she needs to finish her work. He knows she is lovingly dismissing him to his own thoughts. This had always been her strategy to evoke some self-reflection in Jorge. Jorge believes this is one trait different from his father. Unsure if he actually feels remorse for treating Sue badly or merely angry he cannot get her to surrender to his charm. He knows the latter is most likely, but hopes beyond hope there is an ounce of human empathy in his being. It is scary to think he may actually merely be a reincarnate of his heartless father. He is determined this cannot and will not be the case.

CHAPTER 10

Sue decides she needs to stop by the office and clear up any questions the team may have before she leaves to Baltimore, Maryland. It is about a 6-hour drive and if she leaves before noon, she should be there by dinner. Her mother is supposed to be at the Norfolk Carnival Cruise ship by 7am and her boyfriend is supposed to meet her there. She will only have to put up with her mother for a short evening. She is sure she will have to leave at 3am so she will probably go to bed by 8:30pm, calculating only a short 2½ hours with her mother. She can tolerate her for that short length of time, and she will be there 5 days, and get on the road by early Sunday morning, missing her mother's return trip. She can handle it and will enjoy seeing her sisters. She has not seen their new house since her mother moved to Baltimore.

Reflections

Supposedly Sam moved there so the girls would get a better education, but truth be known, she was gold digging. She thought she would land George, an attorney she met while assisting him in the sports gear section of Wal-Mart. He was fishing with his business partners on Lake Erie and needed some particular lures. She is the expert on lures, well not exactly fishing lures…. He had a fling with her and came to town several times, and she went to visit him at least 3 or 4 times. He mentioned she could transfer to the Wal-Mart close by his home. He neglected to tell her he was married. Sam up-rooted the girls during their sophomore and Junior year, following her work transfer. Their dad paid enough child support to get her over the hump and the girls were at an age when they seldom saw their father, so he didn't press the issue.

Sam apparently thought she had George in her clutches, when one evening she was told the shift was overscheduled and she could leave early. She decided to stop by his house. Poor Sam, she stopped in the 50% sale area and bought a sexy Wal-Mart dress, sort of an oxymoron. She was ready to spend a surprise evening with, the "love of her life." She knocked on the door, greeted by a tall, attractive blonde-haired person. She asked if George was home.

The lady said to her husband, "Honey there is some woman from Wal-Mart here, did you leave your wallet or something?"

Sam suddenly realized she had taken off her Wal-Mart uniform, but put on her sweater that had her nametag on it. Still…unwilling to even consider defeat, instead of leaving, like any normal human would do; she stayed long enough to suffer humiliation. Of course in her mind, she dumped him, but truth be known, he came to the door, grabbed her by her arm, asked her, "What the hell are you doing coming to my home and harassing me?"

She told him, "I knew you were married and just thought I would embarrass you."

He slammed the door and she drove home restructuring the story line, convincing herself she didn't need or want him anyway. After all, he was balding.

**

Arriving at the office, Sue grabs her purse and throws on a little lipstick. She is in her travel clothes, a blue workout outfit, with her Nike tennis shoes. Since her morning run, Ginger, her running buddy, has not left her side, whining every time she nears the door. She instinctively knows, with the suitcase out, Sue is going somewhere. Sue opted to get ready and rather than leaving Ginger with her neighbor, she decides to take her. She is a good travel companion, and it is a little comforting to have a protective dog with her. Ginger has to stay in the car, but the weather is beautiful, so with the window rolled down, she will be fine. Her sisters love dogs and when she Face Times with them, they both oooh and awww saying they will love to meet Ginger. Mother never allowed them to have pets. That way, she could always use a pet as a promising advantage for the next obligation or manipulation. Sue pities her mother's ignorance of how she is likely to find herself alone, without children to exploit. Knowing her, in her own mind, there would inevitably be some gullible male to enslave to her wiles.

Sue exits the car, and Ginger is content sticking her nose out the window. She sees Diane about 10 feet in front of her and hollers out, "Hey girl, wait a minute, how was the movie last night?"

Diane stops in her tracks, she thought Sue was leaving this morning and wasn't coming to the team meeting. She feels the blood rushing to her face, latent with guilt from her own thoughts and intentions; she stumbles at her own words, "I didn't think you were coming in this morning. Aren't you going to see your sisters?"

Sue looks at her best friend inquisitively, "Why, you look embarrassed? If I didn't know better, I would say you had a fling with a married man last night?" Responding half seriously, Sue caringly, grabs her friend by the arm and says, "You have to stop having those rendezvous. Yes, they are safe because there are no commitments, but who knows, you may actually get your heart broken one of these days and then I would have to kick his ass, because that is what best friends do!" A smile creeps on Diane's face, she had completely forgotten about Bob, her one nightstand she romped with about 2 months ago. He was unhappily married and fell head over heels for Diane. She chewed him up and spit him out. It was brutal. That is why she forgot all about it yesterday when her temptress was about to jump on Jorge. It hadn't been 6 months after all, what was she thinking?

She relaxes and chuckles, 'No, I wasn't out with a married man. *Only your ex-boyfriend,* her moral self-reminds her. "I was stood up and just ended up drinking a bunch of wine and going to sleep."

"It sounds better than my night of sleeplessness and weird dreams. I am sort of glad to change the routine," Sue says casually as they walk in arm in arm. The team is gathering, getting coffee, chatting about their week schedules.

They turn around as Sue and Diane walk through the door. Jennifer says, "Hey, I thought you were going to visit your sisters? Don't tell me you got ready to go and changed your mind? You deserve to take a little time off, even if it is to go see your sisters."

"No, I am going, I just want to check and make sure everything is coordinated for the week. You know as the team manager, your success is my success. Unfortunately, your loss is mine too, so I wanna make sure we all have a win/win week, despite me not being here," Sue says reassuringly.

Robert chimes in, "What's up with the micromanagement? Life so chaotic, you gotta make sure we are all on course?" He is half joking, and playing with a twinge of sarcastic truth, and Sue realizes she is treating them like her children rather than colleagues on the same team.

She quickly changes her strategy and says, "No, really I just came to get my heavier jacket I left since it is supposed to be a bit colder in Maryland."

They all clear their throats, not succumbing to her renege. She surrenders and sits down, lets them describe their plan. She is confident and knows they will manage without her quite well. She gets up to leave, and Randall gets up quietly, walking to the back of the office, flings his hair back, and dramatically says, "Didn't you forget something Sue? I mean, it was the reason you came to the office?" Sue turns red and everyone laughs, at first, a couple of snorts, then it becomes contagious, and everyone is laughing. Gail attempts to hold in her giggle and takes a sip of coffee with it going down the windpipe, and spews it all over the table. That was it, by this time, the entire team been injected with hysterical laughter. Falling over on her chair, Diane grabs Sue's arm to keep her up, and both of them tumble down to the floor. Legs straight up in the air, they roll over, tears of camaraderie; pour down their faces along with smearing mascara. The *little one*, is startled by the jostling womb, awakens, being flooded with fun chemicals, feelings of happiness and belongingness move through her being.

"Well, that was an experience," Sue says to Ginger as she gets into the car. Ginger whines and Sue gets back out and puts the leash on Ginger, taking her potty before the long drive. Ginger sniffs here and there, taking her own sweet time to find just the right spot to do her duty. Sue doesn't expect her to poop since she took a dump on their run and she responsibly had her poop scoop bag and gloves. She had packed some, but they were way down in her backpack. She sighs frustrated with having to dig out the baggie and disposable gloves. She digs deeply into the bag. She hears the seam tear.

Oh no, she thinks to herself. This bag is her good luck bag. She had it since she was five, and only used it when she felt she really needed luck. Her father had bought it for her on that last trip. It was made of colorful weaved material, and he said it was made by the Seminole Indian Tribe, that was the tribe his mother's ancestors were from. She reaches further down in the bag and feels something on the side she grazes with her fingertips. She fumbles to pick it out of the bag thinking it may be an old piece of discarded candy or something. Instead, she pulls out a smooth rock about an inch in diameter. Her father had given it to her, as he found one just like it as they had been skipping stones in a small creek the morning before the police had taken him away.

He had told her, "Every time you need me, just rub the rock and I will sense you need me." Almost as if it was toxic, rather than rubbing it, she sticks it in her coat pocket and quickly shifts her attention to gathering poop piles and heading down the road.

She loads Ginger into the car and settles in for the drive. Her mother begins her relentless texting. 'Have you left yet? You are not going to let me down are you? The girls are excited…" "Drive careful… I can't wait to see you." Sue seldom feels empowered with her mother, so she doesn't respond, letting her mother go through the myriad of emotions, knowing eventually it will end in desperate, benign threats. For now, she is mused by reading the predictable progression of tactics. *First, there is love and concern. Next, there will be guilt*…Oh, yes… "Sue, you know this trip is paid for and cost a lot of money? You know how hard I work, and raised these girls on my own, I desperately need some time off. It was so hard to raise you right. I know I didn't always do such a good job. I know you probably hate me for all the things you went through.' *Oh, when she uses that one, usually anger follows. Yup, here it comes…* 'You are a worthless ungrateful, arrogant Bitch. I have given my life for you and you move away. How selfish are you.' The last one of course, is threats… Sue decides to play the script all the way out. Oddly enough, it is the only sense of power she has with her mother. Predictably… *have her out of control in a dire attempt to control.* The envelope on the message icon sits idle and Sue's mind wanders to Jorge.

Was that why she ran from with Jorge?… *He attempted to bully her and then apologize?* A sinking feeling tugs at her heart. *Was he a male version of her mother?* She has read about things like this. She was so determined, after reading John Bradshaw's book, as well as Facing Love Addictions: Giving yourself the Power to Change, by Pia Mellody, that there is no way she will repeat history. She is feeling almost sick to her stomach reminded that he is the father of her child. *Is this baby the spawn of Satan?* The fetus recoils inside of her, feeling toxic rejection, unlike any she has experienced since first acknowledged. She protests her feelings, and beckons Source to let her return to her Celestial home.

Sue begins to cramp and grabs her stomach, instinctively repenting for her vile thoughts. She says aloud, "I am so sorry, I know that no matter how your father is, you have me, and I will help you. I had a loving daddy, and I know how that feels. I will love you and take care of you. We can change this life script." Tears trickle down her cheek and she puts her hand in her pocket, deliberately rubbing her stone. At that moment, she receives another text from her mother. Rather than the next stage, a predictable threat, her mother actually apologizes, 'I know you are probably driving and can't text me back. I am sorry for saying those things to you. Your sisters are getting on my last nerves and I think I am going through the change of life. Please just let me know if you are on your way.'" With this reasonable request, Sue takes a moment to say, 'Yes, mother, I am on my way. I have only driven about 2 hours. I will be there by 6 or so. Either we can go out to eat, or we can eat at home. Whatever you decide is fine. Please don't text me anymore as I am driving," she hits send and shuts down the volume to vibrate.

Reflections

She needs to just turn on the radio and jam out to some Classic Rock. Scanning for a local station, she listens to a song by Steven Curtis Chapman called "Cinderella." It takes her back to her father twirling her around and around in the living room, as they danced and swayed together to "Butterfly Kisses, by Bob Carlisle" She smiles nostalgically to herself remembering how safe she felt in her father's arms. She wonders how safe this baby will feel raised by a single parent. She will certainly be more attentive to the selection of men in her life.

**

CHAPTER 11

Ms. DeBoe, feeling agitated, is working on her latest plans on the new Roar on Shore project. She has several local contacts pushing her to utilize their furnishings since it will gain them notoriety as well as local patrons. She finds herself becoming more impatient with Maria, she needs her to make a clear commitment to this position and then take the load off her shoulders. She buzzes her to come into her office. Maria is preoccupied in changing some of the stores display cases and setting in the new spring line of clothing and accessories. She hears the buzz on her store phone and knows when the store phone buzzes she needs to promptly respond. Ms. DeBoe is gracious, but short fused.

Maria walks into her office, with a measuring tape wrapped around her mid-section and a pencil behind her ear. Ms. DeBoe is amused that Maria literally embodies her work. "I haven't heard a definitive answer to the position I offered you several weeks ago. The project has already begun and I have numerous people breathing down my neck. Honestly, I need someone to take this burden off me. Let me know if you cannot take the position so I can find someone else. Of course, I prefer to have you because I know your quality of work and you know and understand my expectations as well as my temperament," she says waiting for a response.

Maria stands there speechless. She presumed there was a tentative agreement, but upon consideration, did not remember signing it into practical and legal job description, as well as compensation. "I am so sorry; I thought you knew I was taking the job. I had no idea you already had the process up and rolling. Although, Dios mio, yo puedo saber…" Maria sometimes resorts to Spanish whenever she is nervous or flustered.

"Slow down, and try to speak English," responds Ms. DeBoe.

"I have been making plans about how to get out of my home situation based on this new position, and it never dawned on me, we had not solidified the position. I am very sorry, lo siento."

"Well, I have the paperwork sitting in front of me on my desk, and if you would review it and sign it, you could take over the brewing mess converging on my head," she says as she reaches for the papers on her desktop.

Maria cringes, but knows she has to put this off for a bit. "Ms. Deboe, I am in the middle of showing Sarah how to measure a design display, and she is supposed to be my replacement. Sarah is standing by the front display looking like a deer with headlights on its horns..."

Ms. DeBoe interrupts her, "That is a deer in headlights... the phrase is about a deer standing in the middle of the road and a car is coming and blinds it, so it cannot see where to go..." She finds it amusing and annoying when Maria attempts to use metaphors and butchers them.

"Well, she should not be out there looking that way, she will scare off the customers," Maria says with conviction.

Ms. DeBoe tells her to come in during lunch and review the position, and if in agreement, she needs to sign the paperwork and begin immediately.

Maria without more ado heads out to rescue Sarah from her own demise. The customers here tend to be a bit snide. Women who have nothing better to do than to find fault with anything that has two legs, is attractive, and has a vagina. Sarah Sabeans meets all the qualities, with long blonde hair, perfect figure, dressed immaculately, and is naïve to her job position. She is French, and Maria enjoys that. She just graduated with a Master's degree in Fashion design, but went straight through school with little real life experience. She definitely has the knowledge and knack for color and design; however, she has never been fully responsible for real store displays. She always had perfectly contoured spaces, and dimensions set for typical settings. Ms. DeBoe made her stores famous for creating uncanny depths perceptions and non-symmetrical spaces. Maria had experience when working in her father's store because his space was limited, so she became creative using backdrops and floating displays, with several tiers. If the truth be known, it wasn't Ms. DeBoe's designs, but Maria's that made DeBoe famous. She knew it and DeBoe knew it, and Ms. DeBoe will pay handsomely to keep Maria around.

A couple of the vultures are fixing to set in and go for the kill when Maria arrives just in time. Mrs. Anderson, a prominent Republican African American State Representative, asks Sarah, "What in the world are you intending on doing with the undressed mannequin?" Extending the question with a snide comment, "I guess with these young liberal women, they are going to let our children think nudity is the newest style, only to be draped by a scarf or two."

Maria, used to their antics says, "Hello Ms. Anderson, I told Sarah you may be by today and would have some great ideas about setting the stage for the spring ware. You think the mannequin should have on a nice spring dress or a conservative spring pants outfit?" Of course, using the word conservative, set the decision, and Maria already had that in mind. "Now, if you will excuse us, we need to finish the display."

Sarah hears Mrs. Anderson saying, "I just love that Maria, and she sure knows how to put those young things in place. It is too bad she is Latino. She may make a better politician than her husband. We just don't have any more room for more minorities right now in the House."

Maria shows Sarah how to measure the mannequin from the side, and narrow her stance, giving her a profile position, while she sets another mannequin on a ledge right above her. With legs and feet dangling, these mannequins are costlier because every joint is flexible allowing for versatility of positioning. The display is magic, it looks real and the clothing dramatically enhanced with pots of flowers, and swirls of paint in the background. Sarah seems to pick up well on the process and is able to complete two other display cases herself. Finally, Maria makes a call to Ms. DeBoe to look and see if she approves of Sarah's work. The decision is easy to make, as numerous people walk into the store admiring the display and purchasing the matching clothing line. She muses as she notes the women at the register. She knows these women, and as soon as they wear their clothing to the next outing, it will inspire a competition in at least 10 other women; who will then come in to purchase a different style of the same named designer.

She is as pleased as she can be, and tells Maria to go review the papers, while she speaks to Sarah. Sarah, hearing the rumors of Ms. DeBoe's temper, looks helplessly at Maria. Maria smiles... She knows Ms. DeBoe is pleased and Sarah is going to see the side of Ms. DeBoe that makes it worthwhile to work for her. She puts her arm over Sarah's shoulders, and walks her around the store recounting the entire DeBoe image. Maria feels satisfied she has hired the right person to take her place while she begins her new venture on the Roar on Shore project, and to get away from her husband.

Maria considers Sarah, as she notices a crucifix on her silver necklace, and is curious if she could really be as sweet as she comes across to be? *Wow...educated, beautiful, and sweet. How great would it be for Jorge to go out with a Dulce Belleza (sweet beauty) like Sarah? Maybe she should have Sarah over to work on a project and invite Jorge over for his favorite meal.* She mumbles to herself, *Es hora de nietos (it's time for grandbabies).*

CHAPTER 12

On the Ohio turnpike E listening to her Google map mechanical voice "becomes I-76 E/Pennsylvania Turnpike E," realizing they have traveled almost 160 miles. She is tired, and hungry and Ginger, ready for a stretch. Stepping out of her car, glancing up at one of the shiny trucks, and is reminded of the years gone by. Instinctively, as if it had always been there, she rubs the stone in her pocket. Ginger begins to whine and Sue puts her leash on her, and says, "Ginger, you need to be patient, I have to get my things" and grabs her backpack. Mindlessly she walks Ginger around on the damp newly sprouting grass, with her colorful backpack hanging loosely off her arm.

A truck driver passes by her to mount up the steps on his freshly washed, shiny purple truck. Sue glances at him, and he catches her eyes briefly. She notices the purple on his truck, reminded of the purple plus sign on the pregnancy stick, and realizes she is no longer anxious or repulsed by the thought of motherhood. A slight smile comes to Sue's face and Ginger thinks she is happy with her and wags her tail, despite her continued efforts to find the perfect spot to do her business. The truck driver, settles in his seat, puts on his seatbelt, and from a bird's eye view, notices the girl and her dog. For whatever reason, he glances at the backpack and has a peculiar feeling, but dismisses it as indigestion from the chicken fried steak and gravy he just put down too fast.

Reflections

Back on the road, they settle in, almost half way to their destination, surprised she senses a certain excitement about seeing her younger sisters. How long has it been? Well, she has never seen her mother's home in Maryland, so it has been over a year. Perhaps it was the Christmas before last. She pauses for a moment, recalling that Christmas morning, spending the night at her mother's home. She woke up to her mother yelling at her sister, Sylvia, for taking her flat iron without asking; then watching the flat iron flying past her door and down the stairs, shattering into pieces as she heard it bounced onto the tile hallway, sarcastically saying out loud, "HO HO HO, MERRY CHRISTMAS!"

Her stomach clinching with the thought, and the hotdog, cheese and chili she devoured from the last truck stop didn't help.

Her efforts to shift her thoughts are thwarted as she turns on the radio and "Cats in the Cradle" playing, bring her straight back to thoughts of family. She continues with the relentless memory… She had been away from home two years, so she no longer felt the desire to be the referee in the family dynamics. Sue, determined not to fall back into the old dysfunctional family roles, tried to stay out of it. Unfortunately, she was unable to refrain herself when she heard Sarah jumped in and further screamed at Sylvia for using her eye shadow without asking. The triangulation began… Sue felt ultimately compelled, wiping the sleep from her eyes, grabbing her Santa house shoes; she headed out of the bedroom, and stood between Sylvia, her mother, and Sarah. Lifting her arms, like a referee, she shouted, "Stop it, all of you… It is Christmas morning, and I am sure Jesus would prefer his birthday begin in other ways besides yelling and screaming at each other." She was able to deescalate the conflict, and felt a terrible knot in her gut, as if she had entered into the Twilight Zone. At that moment, she vowed, if possible, she did not want to spend another Christmas with her family… At least this trip is not Christmas.

**

Driving to the address given on her Google maps seems confusing. It is right off Interstate 95, in a quiet, artsy community with what appears to be row houses. She notices the name, Otterbein. She knows living in Maryland is likely to be more money than her mother can afford, but then again, Sue intuitively knows her mother most likely already has her next potential candidate in line, just in case Tom didn't work out. *Perhaps it is one of Tom's friends… better yet, some politician.* Ohhh, her gut twinges, and she bets herself she hit the nail on the head. Maryland is so close to Washington D.C… Perhaps it is a second home. She wonders if this one may be married, also. Her mother is getting older and her selection may be limited. She scolds herself for spending so much time ruminating about her mother.

She has been very successful the last year, and worked to restructure her thoughts when her mind drifts, wondering what her mother is doing and how she is treating the girls. She hates feeling like an abandoning mother to her sisters.

Ginger begins whining, as if she knows exactly where they are going, and telling Sue it is time to stop. Sure enough, there it is 1218 William Ave. She pulls up to a quaint sandy brick row house, with a satellite extending up on the second floor. She knocks on the door, and no one answers, but the door is unlocked. She and Ginger slowly enter, as she quietly hollers, "Mother, Sylvia, Sarah…where are you?" She becomes aware this is a three-tier home, and with Ginger tugging on her lease, she rapidly is lead through an obviously very nicely renovated home with hard wood floors and winding staircases. The wall in the hallway is made of original brick and is very appealing. She finds the small back yard with a small patch of grass, but enough for Ginger to find relief.

About that time, she hears her sister's voices, "Sue, where are you?" They rush through the house and race out the door like a 5 and 6-year-old, but both well over 5'6". One almost jumps in her arms, while the other stops suddenly to bend down and pet Ginger. Sarah, with dark, wavy shoulder length hair, is dressed modestly, and Sylvia, has her hair dyed a deep burgundy, with her makeup in deep shades of pink and purple, with long luscious lashes. She kisses her sister Sylvia and holds her at arm's length, and as a mother would do, she says,

"Wow, you are so grown up… How did that happen? Last time I saw you, you were at least 2 inches shorter!"

Sylvia laughs as she lifts up one of her feet enough for Sue to see she has 3-inch heels on her brown ankle boots. She laughs, "Yeah, these give a good illusion!"

Sarah rises up, looks straight into her sister's eyes, and says, "Why did you let Mother bring us here? We left all our friends, and we left you. Do you not care about us?"

Reflections

Wow, Sue is at a loss for words. She figures her sisters did not want to move, but felt, for once, she did not want to argue with her mother … blamed by her mother, and be made to feel like an idiot for questioning her mother's judgment. Despite how her mother made her feel like a failure and insignificant, every so often, her mother would listen to her. Like when she finally pleaded with her mother to leave Mark before he did to the other girls what he did to her. Her mother did not deny, or apologize for letting him abuse her, but she stopped arguing with her, and left the room. Later, when Sue came home from work, the mother was packed and the girls were in the car. They moved into a quaint apartment, and the child support was significant because Sammie threatened Mark with turning him in for what he did to Sue. Samantha was able to keep her job at Wal-Mart and the girls felt happy and safe in their new environment. That is when her mother began dating George and then Tom just a little later.

* *

She comes to her senses, hearing her mother's voice, "Hello Sue, I decided to go out and grab a pizza, and the girls wanted to make sure I bought your favorite pizza, chicken with Alfredo sauce." Sue's stomach grumbles, and she realizes she is hungry and has a baby to feed. She shudders, as if she spoke the words aloud. Her mother corrals them into the house, and Ginger walks beside Sarah, as if she finds a new best friend. How odd it feels, to be with family. The people Sue has run away from now give her a certain feeling of belonging. Life has its odd twists and turns. She knows she is just beginning some new roadways, and feels unsure if she can handle what lies ahead, but is still unwilling and unable to disclose even the slightest hint to her family.

CHAPTER 13

Jorge, following graduation, goes to work for the Cleveland Heights, Huntington's Bank, as a branch manager. His father defended the bank manager in court and he owed him a favor or two. Jorge has a natural affinity for numbers and so, he has caught on well. It is a reasonable job for the interim while waiting for approval to law school. Besides, he has met so many beautiful women... his contact folder in his cell phone named, "potentials," is growing daily. He is waiting for one of the customers to come in and he scrolls down his list. He notices Sue's number, and tries dialing, once again. He never allows himself to call a girl multiple times. If she does not call him back after once, he will delete the contact. *What is it about Sue? She is attractive, but more than that, there is substance in her.* He can't get her off his mind. It pisses him off, but in a good way. It makes him motivated and driven. He intuitively knows she is not going to answer her phone. He remembers on the fourth ring that Diane told him she was going to see her sisters this week. It doesn't matter; he will win her because he knows how to get what he wants. His father taught him well. He hears a knock on his office door and his next client arrives, and he lets his plan simmer.

Diane feels exhausted after working the extra hours for Sue while she is out of town. They had an agreement If Diane would keep the team directed, motivated, and sales up, then Sue would share half of the manager's commission. She was unaware of how much work it is to be a manager, but she can see it is worth it. The higher income is about $750.00 more a month. Hmm, she thinks perhaps she can consider advancing to management. Somewhere in the recesses of her mind, she remembers a guy Sue told her about, and believes she has his name in her phone. She looks for his number but cannot quite remember his name. For some reason, she believes it starts with a J... *what is it?* She sees Jace, James, Jess...no Jack. *What is his last name?* She thinks to herself, *It is a simple, almost stupid name... is it Jack Jones? Jack Johnson? Jack Joe? No, it is ...hummm...Jack Jill.* She laughs, *yes, that is it...like Jack and Jill.*

She puts on her blue suede jacket since the spring evenings still hold some chill in the evening. She is sitting at Sue's desk and has access to all of the manager's charts in the file cabinet. Sue gave Diane her work keys including the file cabinet. Her temptress self is in full blossom, as she finds Jack's file. She sits on the edge of the desk, and tugs on her skirt and slides her hand up and down her tan thigh. She reads the file and has difficulty with deciphering company rating and testing. It makes her head hurt as she attempts to find the demographics. She flips through the pages and finally comes across Jack Jill's phone number. She figures, *Why not? He may be home… It appears he is divorced.* She yawns, as she dials his number and realizes she is tired, hungry and bored. Jenn walks by, noticing Diane in the files.

The phone rings three times and she is about to hang up and rest her plan for the night, when she hears a voice on the other end. "Hello, Jack speaking, how can I help you?" He says in a pseudo sexy voice.

Caught off guard, Diane catches her thoughts, and slowly replies, "Uhh, hello Jack, this is Diane from Kirby…I am on Sue's team. Remember, the one with the red Voltzwagon who almost ran into you the other day coming out of the parking lot?"

He chuckles, and states, "Oh yes, I jumped out of my Mercedes and was furious. I was going to give you a word or two when I saw you shaking as you looked up. I couldn't get mad when I looked into those lovely blue eyes."

Well, this was going to be easier than she thought. Diane states, "I was so impressed you didn't yell at me… a true gentleman… a quality sort of guy. That is exactly the reason I am calling you. I need a little help. I am filling in for Sue as team manager and I could use some advice from a Senior Manager."

He thinks to himself, *she is pretty cute, I think we can help each other…. I could use a little female company tonight.* He clears his throat, "I have a pretty busy evening scheduled, but I may be able to clear calendar to meet you somewhere for a while." Both feel they have hooked one another in for the bait, and the set up begins. The question is, will each one win, or lose?

Diane agrees to meet Jack for dinner at Mr. Peabody's Grill off the Outerbelt S. freeway. She likes the sports bar environment, with flat screens and booths. It has been awhile since she has played pool and if Jack becomes too handsy, she can challenge him to a game of pool. She has to go home and change into some skinny jeans, black sweater, and black ankle boots. She gets a last look at herself in the large round mirror in the hallway, putting on some crimson red lipstick, and spiking up her hair a few more strokes. She hears her phone ring thinking it must be Jack confirming their work date. "I should be there in about 20 minutes, Jack," she says hurriedly.

"Hey, Diane, this isn't Jack, this is Jorge."

Diane suddenly feels lightheaded with pressure in her chest. She has wondered if, and when Jorge will get back with her. "Oh, Jorge, how are you? I have thought about you numerous times and wondered about how you are doing?" Diane stumbles with her words. She can feel the electricity through the phone.

"Well," Jorge states, "I was hoping you may be hungry and want to catch a bite to eat with me?"

"Uhh, well I was just about to go and meet one of the Senior Managers for a work date at Mr. Peabody's and grab some food while we talk some business," Diane hesitates. She does not want to miss an opportunity with Jorge. She feels the heat and moisture create a female yearning, and the plan with Jack seems much less significant.

Jorge interrupts her thoughts, as if he was reading her like a book. "Really, sometimes I go to Mr. Peabody's to play in the pool tournament… Perhaps I could show up and play some pool until you are done with your work meeting. We can catch a few drinks afterwards?"

That does it, he loves pool, too… gorgeous, athletic, smart… does it matter my best friend is pregnant with his child? Diane attempts desperately to justify her lust filled thoughts and feelings towards Jorge. *I have known him longer, we have a history, I can help him to detach from Sue by telling him some of her history. She is the one that has emphatically said she does not want him in her life. What else are best friends for?*

She now has to re-navigate her plan, leaving some room for Jack, but making her primary focus on Jorge. Her temptress moves her back to the mirror to highlight her eyes with deeper richer mascara, and a creamy blue sparkling eye shadow. Her eyes look like a Persian cat and she feels like a cat on the prowl for her prey… *two victories in one night!* Can she pull this off successfully? Her phone rings again, this time she hears her special best friend ringtone… It is Sue. She debates whether to pick up the phone or not. She lets it go to voicemail and decides she will listen to it later and deal with any residual guilt, but now, she has her agendas and the thrill of the evening ahead seeps into her psyche. She wonders if this is what her mother experiences when she knows she may have a rendezvous with several couples at a time. Diane feels a twinge of her conscience and a sort of sick feeling about the genetic or generational influence. She stops her ruminations as she gets into her car and turns on some light rock music.

Before she realizes it, she is pulling up to Mr. Peabody's grill. She is surprised the parking lot is not completely full since it is basketball season, and usually the bar is full. She parks her Volkswagen and glances one last time in her rear view mirror. She looks into her big blue eyes and can almost see her internal conflicts as she feels betrayal of a friendship is blooming as sure as the flowers in May. Is it legitimate for her to try to push for Sue's position, knowing her job may be at risk with her pregnancy? Is it legitimate for her to want to land Jorge in bed just as soon as possible, knowing he is the father to Sue's baby? It is like a deep-rooted compulsion burning inside. She has a vague memory of this morning at work, when Jennifer made some comment about, "Whatever a person sows, that is what they will reap." She muses to herself… *Jenn is the workplace evangelist.* What would she say if she could read Diane's thoughts today? She shudders at the thought. Jenn would probably tell her she is going to hell in a hand basket... *whatever that phrases means; it must be for bad people.* She has been fighting these demons for years, and she feels the tug of war in her soul. She is about to engage at a point of no return. A voice inside of her warns her, but her temptress is ruthless. She shakes her head, as if to stop the argument in her soul.

Diane walks into the front door with the decor NASCAR and Cleveland sports with hard wood accents, and immediately notices the balding head, and the grey suit sitting at the bar. She is relieved he is not at a table since the tables have the most uncomfortable chairs "like something out of a medieval torture dining set with straight backs that crushed your spin," she remembers reading that on Yelp and laughing until she actually sat in the chairs. From then on, the bar stools were her choice. Looking at Jack, she laughs to herself; noticing he has overdressed for the location... her stomach feels queasy. She walks up and slips into the barstool next to him and he stands up and holds her hand to his lips saying, "Wow, don't you look lovely Diane. Looking at you gives me a change in appetite." She glances at him up and down as if measuring cost versus risk. Sue had told her how Jack had come onto her and how disgusted she was with him. She can know exactly why as she sees his pearly white fake smile and his buttons about to pop on his pressed dress shirt.

She attempts to disregard his seduction attempts, and says, "Well, I can now understand why management is such a valued position. This week, since I have taken Sue's place on the team, I realize how difficult it is to keep track of routes, schedules, and motivation of team members."

Jack, putting on the air of superiority, thinks that perhaps positional power is his best approach, "You are absolutely correct and it has taken me many years of strategic learning to get to the pinnacle of my career."

Diane feels unsettled in what she even hopes to gain from this deluded narcissistic frump. She changes the subject to food, "I am starving, and I hope you haven't eaten yet." She does love the wings and orders a bottle of Bud Light and a dozen spicy Buffalo wings. Jack had already ordered a burger, so the orders came out close together. He tries to play footsy with her will she tries to eat.

Jack says, "It is obvious you need or want my help with something, but what can you offer me for my experience and efforts if I choose to help you out?" *Wow, there really wasn't much gaming here; he just gets straight to the point!* Diane dismally thinks to herself.

"Well, I thought it would look good to corporate if they knew you were training their underlings to move up the ladder," Diane says, hoping it will hit his vanity the right way.

"Contrary, corporate doesn't need more upper management to pay higher amounts to, and in fact, discourages us in Senior management to have the sales team pursue higher positions. If I assist someone, I have to see what is in it for me, if you know what I mean. I did offer to help Sue at one point, but she is stubborn, and said she could do it on her own. I offered to help her because the team she was pursuing as a team manager had done so poorly the last two years, and they would be directly affecting my income if I could get them at higher volumes of sales. I have to admire her; she has worked hard and now has a hell of a team, including you. However, for now, I am at top gain, and don't need or have any other teams to build. Especially if it means someone who hasn't earned it, is attempting to supersede those who have done their due diligence." He looks into her eyes as if he is reading her soul. She is at a loss for words. Should she tell him Sue is pregnant and things will likely change soon?

She hears his words, and is engrossed in her thoughts, thinking of her friend, Sue. How admired she is, and she has done a great job, what is she thinking trying to steal her position out from under her? She notices a commotion at the pool table, as there is some whoops and hollers, glancing over, there he is, Jorge. He is holding his mug of beer up to cheer someone. He must have just won a game. She had almost forgotten he told her he would be at the pool tables. She mindlessly wipes her mouth off, excuses herself from Jack, and walks over to the pool table. Jack chuckles to himself, *Guess I am not getting any tonight*, as he sees Diane walk up to Jorge. Jack may not be the brightest, but he intuitively knows he does not stand a chance against someone who looks like Jorge, especially if he just told Diane he wasn't going to help her unless she meets his needs. He feels a little stupid and arrogant now that he sees Jorge twirl her around in a spin… *More than an acquaintance?… Hummm?* He belches at no one, but at the situation. He finishes his burger, pays in cash and heads back home. *Oh well, it was a little exciting and broke the monotony of the evening.*

CHAPTER 14

John, fatigued, arrives home after having a couple of drinks with his partner, Bob. He is feeling disturbed because Bob has been expressing resistance to him taking time away from the firm to do some campaigning. John believes he needs to get in touch with the people and gain lobbying power through becoming more familiar with some of the situations the locals are facing. He initially assumes being a prominent attorney would suffice in his campaign. In his understanding, his father had been involved in the Republican Senate through having a thriving Law Practice. To this point, that theory has not proven true. His father never explained much to him, but pushed him towards law school with an unspoken expectation John would follow with politics.

Reflections

His father, John Senior, was a brutal man who would not allow John junior to play sports or run in track, the two things John wanted more than anything. Instead, he had to make good grades, be involved in Student Council, Model UN and debate. John senior would not listen to John's pleas for sports. John could not stand to see his father brutalize his mother and sisters, and run around on his mother, so he began working full time as a junior in high school. He was in AP classes, and would stay at the library half the night to keep up with his studies. His mother was sickly and frail, and from a British background, making her appear somewhat aloof. They attended a stuffy Presbyterian Church, with primarily white Caucasian republicans.

When he met Maria at the University, taken aback by her beauty, skin, accent, and mostly feeling the independent rebellion to do something his father would hate, and have no control over. To marry a Hispanic design major!!! They dated a few months and his father threatened his college tuition, his car, etc. However, he had too much bragging power over what John had done thus far, to follow through on his idle threats. Despite the resistance, his parents gave into the wedding plans, and as long as they did not marry at a Catholic Church, they were happy. Maria was rebellious to her father's catholic control, so she was willing to have a wedding at a local chapel, really a renovated mansion, called Mansion on the Lake, with the pastor provided. The wedding was frilly with a flare of colors reflecting Maria's Hispanic culture, but his parents catered the reception with a stiff orchestra rather than Mariachis.

Both were young and rebellious, looking for a way to get out of parental clutches and create a unique family. It was wonderful when Maria found out she was pregnant. However, John, as he reflects on their early relationship realizes something changed in him, almost as soon as he found out Maria was pregnant. He began to become extremely jealous and possessive. He would drink too much and take his frustrations out on Maria. Prior to the pregnancy, he had admired what a spitfire she was, and she would not tolerate a moment of his dominance. Nevertheless, when she found out, she was pregnant; she was more guarded and protective, giving into John's tirades, for fear of him hurting her and her losing the baby.

He went to work as an intern at his father's firm, and was extremely miserable, with his father's demanding and unrelenting criticism. His father would tell him if he had a granddaughter then not to even invite him to the birth. Shortly after that, he found out they were having a boy. He was ambivalent in his feelings about his son. He was happy he was having a son, but on the other hand, angry he was giving his father what he wanted.

From the time, Jorge was small; his mother noticed his artistic flair and musical talent. It made John mad, and he would take Jorge away from his piano, paint palate, or any other expressive modality, and get him outside to groom him in sports. He became obsessed with him playing sports, especially when his father, John Senior would come over and comment, "What are you doing, creating a Jock? You know it took all of my power to keep you out of that shit, and look where you are now!"

He remembers when his life changed forever, Jorge was 6 years old, Maria had been gone, and he had not been able to get in touch with her. The school called him to come and pick up Jorge who was in the office sick. John was in an important meeting and had to leave and pick up Jorge. John, aggravated, he was enraged. He went into the office to find Jorge sitting on the floor coloring and singing a song. He protested having to take him out of school, until Jorge looked up at him with a beet red face, with sweat rolling down. The school nurse said he had been running a fever all day and he had not been able to get in touch with his mother. Maria was always available, and the worst thoughts went through John's mind. He thought she must have been having an affair, so he was ready to show her what happens when people have affairs. As a child, John always wished he could beat the shit out of his father, when he would come home after being gone for several nights. He would hear his mother cry and ask why he had to have other women. He told her she just wasn't enough. John thought Maria didn't think he was enough; he was gone all the time and worked late hours. He grabbed up Jorge, and by the time he got home, he was beside himself. He sent Jorge upstairs, gave him some Tylenol, and waited.

Maria barely walked in the door, and John grabbed her arm and flung her around. She lost her balance and tripped, crashing over the end table and landing on a pile of law books in the living room. Her face hit the ledge of the fireplace and she busted her lip. She was in shock, and looked up at John in horror. He accused her of everything other than having sex with his father, who she hated. He can't remember what he actually did, but remembers, he later found out she had been at the doctor's office that day and had another pregnancy confirmed. That is, until she lost it later that night. Rushed to the emergency room and while doing a DNC, she began to hemorrhage. To make a bad memory worse, shortly afterwards she had to have a full hysterectomy and thus, Jorge became an only child. From then on, John's shame and love/hate relationship for Jorge increased. Maria went into a severe depression, and while Jorge, was babied and nurtured, Maria began treating John like a stranger in his own home. He began to use more and more power on both of them. The person he swore he would never be like, he resembled more each day.

**

John walks into his home feeling some sense of regret, wishing he had been a little kinder to his family, and is waiting for a wonderful aroma to hit his nostrils. Maria always had food ready especially by 8pm. John had been out with Bob for about an hour and a half and knew she would be back from work at least by 7pm. He notices her hours have changed since she had her promotion, but he is willing to endure the change for the reputation as well as campaign benefit. He has been preoccupied, and realizes he has not had not had sex in over 5 days and he feels his hard cock growing by the moment. He can use a little romp in bed even before he eats dinner.

He walks through the house, calling his wife. The garage is closed as usual. He has not bothered to open it because her recent projects were taking up the other car space. She promised she would only have a couple more weeks of them and he could have his space back. It is spring and so he isn't so worried about having to walk outside to get to his car. He feels a certain sense of panic to go out and look in the garage, but he puts the thought out of his mind, and figures she is upstairs watching T.V. in the room, or reading a book. He feels a certain creepy feeling of loneliness. He is unaccustomed to this sensation, but the sensation increases as he goes into his bedroom, and it seems to feel empty. He looks in Maria's closet, and somehow it seems emptier. He rapidly walks into the bathroom flinging open her makeup cabinet, finding most of her makeup gone. He begins to call out her name, "Maria…where in the hell are you?" 'Hey, I was ready for a good fuck, my love… he nervously laughs…' He runs down the stairs and heads to the garage door, flipping on the light. He stands there looking into the garage, with an empty spot where her car should be.

He feels faint, all the blood draining from his face. He feels afraid. *Where is she, what has happened to her?* He doesn't know what else to do. He pulls his phone out of his pocket and tries to call Maria, only to get a voice that says, "This number is no longer in service at this time." Before he can think, he collapses and feels tears stream down his face. What is happening to him? He has to pull it together, find out where she is. Didn't she say something about an emergency visit to her Aunt in Mexico? He is unsure who to call, but somehow is confident she would have told Jorge where she is.

Jorge feels his phone buzzing in his pocket, but he is having too much fun in his gaming with Diane to answer. He notices her business meeting ended shortly after she came over to say hello. They play a couple of games of pool and she is actually pretty good and won one out of three. She gives him a little information about Sue's family dynamics, letting him know Sue feels overly responsible for her sisters, and has a more than stressed relationship with her mother. It is enough to begin his strategy. After another beer or two, he finally reaches in his pocket and pulls out his phone. He notices 10 calls from his father, and 15 text messages. The messages sound desperate. He sighs realizing his mother must have left and the pressure for his father to find her will become intense. He feels it is better to ignore his calls and act like his phone has been lost or broken. Even more reason to enjoy Diane's company and keep his mind off the inevitable. He looks up and she is smiling seductively. The evening is young! He invites himself to her apartment, and she is absorbed in his myriad of effective tactics to get his way. His smile, teases, and direct and indirect charm has won her over for this evening, or however long he wishes.

Diane sort of floats to her car and opens her door feeling like a giddy schoolchild. She is aware what she is about to do and her seductress is hot and ready to get with it and take full advantage of the evening being young. She reaches into her glove compartment to retrieve her cell phone. She left it in there just in case she needed an excuse to get away from Jack. She can always tell him she is expecting an important call and left her phone in the car. She can call him from the phone, and one of the team members is calling. He understands they do many evening demonstrations and a team manager is sort of on duty 24/7. She noticed several messages from Sue and based on what she saw, and how she had just discussed with Jorge these very dynamics, she felt obligated to read them.

93

"Hey girl, hope the team hasn't caused you too much undo heartache. …Still on the road driving." 5:10pm

"Didn't hear back from you? Got to my mother's home and the girls are blaming me for them having to move here. They thought I should have helped them talk Sam out of it. I knew they didn't want to move out again… but I can't control that woman! BTW…I just needed to vent." 7:15pm

"The girls aren't as bad as I thought… They love Ginger, and they have hardly left my side. Sam has been busy finishing her packing. There hasn't been any pandemic criticism…guess Samantha is afraid I might just walk out on her the last minute if she gives me grief. I wish I could do something like that, but I would hate to disappoint the girls. They have enough daily disappointments living with the biache… lol" 8pm

"Where are you?" 8:15pm

"Sam came in and announced she was going to bed and everyone needs to BE QUIET! The girls burst out in laughter, rather reminded me of this morning at the office. BTW… was something wrong? You seemed aloof in the parking lot, and before I was leaving and handed you the key, you seemed very tense. Is everything O.K.?" 8:35pm

Reading the texts, Diane realizes it is now 9pm and she is sitting in the parking lot of her apartments. She had become pre-occupied fretting over what she was contemplating. Upon reading the texts from Sue, Diane is actually feeling a little relief for having a conscience about this situation. She considers her options while she contemplates what to do next. She decides it sounds like her friend needs her, so she texts her back.

TEXT RESPONSE: "Met with Jack, our senior team manager… remember the balding one? He wanted to check on my progress with your team since he knew you were out of town. I guess you can guess what he really wanted. He couldn't keep his hands off of me. Luckily, I was saved from his clutches when I say Jorge playing pool. I was able to excuse myself from Jack, and then try to figure out what Jorge wanted when he called to talk to you the other day… I am always watching your back… What are BFF's for anyway?" 9:05pm

Reflections

Sue is dumbfounded. She doesn't know what to make of this text response from Diane. She met with Jack? Why would Jack be checking up on her? She had missed a few days from morning sickness, but the team number of sales was about the same as last month. Maybe he has heard her puking and figured out she is pregnant? Surely Diane would not give this secret out? It will be obvious soon enough… She tries to live with the philosophy, "Don't borrow sorrow," and this secret without a strategic plan, could wreak havoc on her life.

On second thought, it has already caused some chaos, at least inside of her, and certainly put a damper on her relationship with Jorge. Whatever sort of relationship that has been… What is a month long relationship, anyway? Then to find out you are pregnant… most likely THE VERY FIRST TIME… *what sort of sick irony do the celestial gods have against her?* Her questions reel unrelentingly, growing from bad to worse. *Where is Diane now? Did she talk to Jorge? Did she tell him anything? Did she find out anything?*

* *

She cannot help herself… she has to call. The girls are in watching T.V. She heard them talking about a new sitcom called, "Broke Girls." She is amused at the title. She has had definite times in life where she could relate to that theme. She picks up her phone to call Diane, when Sylvia runs into her room and leaps into her bed with her.

"Gonna sleep with you," she announces. As Sue is just about to protest, another body flies the bed.

"Me too!" exclaims the younger sister. So much for calling Diane, she sighs to herself. She has to put her curiosity to rest, because the girls are ALL EARS.

Jorge has some moments to reflect, something he seldom does. He thinks back on the evening and realizes Diane became overtly sexual with her tight jeans, coquettish demeanor, and consistent touching and flirtation. Wasn't that what he wanted and expected? What was eating him anyway? He remembers his mother and one of the last heart- to- heart talks he had with her. She pleaded with him to stop treating women like objects. He can hear his mother's gentle but firm voice, "tratar a su amor como una rosa fragante," (treat your love like a fragrant rose).

As he drives towards Diane's apartment, he realizes there is nothing about her that he loves. He certainly cannot see himself treating her like a fragrant rose! Of course, she does have a nice body. He has to stop his testosterone filled male slut from speaking. Instead, as quickly as the thought/feeling enters his mind, he picks up his cell phone.

"Hello Diane," he speaks rapidly knowing his mind is easily changed. Diane sees the MALE SLUT name flash on her caller ID and is afraid he arrived at the apartment before her and already left. She chose to take a different route, hoping it would be faster, instead, there were detours, two lanes reduced to one lane, and more stoplights than she had remembered. She is just about to speak out her excuse, with the hope Jorge will come back. Before she has time to speak, Jorge dismisses the evening. He gives some lame excuse of his mother needing him.

She feels miserable and hates the fact she feels so ambivalent. On one hand, as Sue's BFF, she is relieved Jorge did not end up spending the night with her; however, the temptress feels insulted this was his second time to change his mind. She feels almost nauseated to know she is eventually going to end up bringing her toy box out from under the bed to give her some sensual relief. She is done with Jorge and his player antics!

Jorge justifies standing Diane up; after all, he sort of heard his mother's voice in his head, and really needs to talk to her, better yet, to see her. It is early enough to see if she is somewhere in the city.

Meanwhile, John, Jorge's father, tries to track Jorge's whereabouts through his phone but notices the locator is off. He is obsessed with finding Maria. He tries calling her father, and even pays him a visit. Of course, he is nice at first. His father in law denies knowing her whereabouts for sure, but assumes she has gone to Mexico to visit her mother's sister. John is aware of the family feud related to Maria's aunts. He knows her father stays as far away from that family drama as possible. It is believable for him to say he does not know exactly what is going on there since he refuses to ask his wife anything about her sister!

He hates to pull the strategies he often recommends to his clients, but after he could not keep track of Jorge, he pays his PI to follow Jorge as well as put a tracking device on his vehicle. Jorge is unaware his father is having him followed and while he is in the pub, the device is installed. Jorge does not think anything about parking in the alley close by the Pub. The PI had been following him the last day or two. Parking in the alley gives him the perfect opportunity to put the tracker on unnoticed.

Jorge attempts to call his mother's phone from his cell and hears, "This number is not in service at this time." He is a bit confused, but then remembers, she told him to use the other pre-paid phone he put in his truck. He reaches into his armrest, and pulls out the phone. It has a paper taped to it and it said, ~Call this number if you need me for anything urgent. ~

He calls the number and Maria answers, "I didn't figure you would get right back with me until your father contacted you. Has he already contacted you, or are you just bored with no available female tonight?"

Ouch that hurt! "No, in fact Mi Mamá, I stood one up tonight just to find a few moments with mi Madre Preciósa," he humorously retorts.

She proclaims, "Gracias a Dios."

Maria begins to sense this is perhaps a divine intervention. She currently is working on a project with Sarah and she has been praying about Jorge meeting Sarah. She ponders multiple ways to have him randomly meet her but knew as soon as Jorge saw her he would know she was up to her matchmaking tactics. Ever since High School, Jorge has been going out with "loose women" and Maria wants him to meet a beautiful NICE girl. She feels excited inside, and knows this is her opportunity. "Jorge, can you stop by and see me for a while. I am working in one of the warehouses and am starving. I haven't eaten since noon," she requests pleadingly. She is aware Jorge has a soft spot for getting his mother food when she asks, probably from all the wonderful meals she historically prepared for him. *Guess motherhood has its benefits on occasion.*

CHAPTER 15

"Wake up…gotta go in 20 minutes. Coffee is on… Throw your clothes on!" says Sam. Samantha has turned on the lights and is fully dressed hovering over Sue and the girls.

"What time is it?" Sue sleepily asks.

"It is 3:15am and we gotta go. I don't want to be late for the cruise ship," says Samantha, "and besides, Tom has already called and said he is heading out."

Sue realizes there is no arguing with her mother, and besides, the sooner she drops her off, the sooner she will be free of her company… a small price to pay for peace of mind and some alone time with her sisters.

The two sisters roll over and mumble "Good bye" to their mother, and "See you later" to Sue. Sue groggily grabs her first cup of coffee and they are on the road by 3:30am, about the time Sue anticipated her mother would want to leave.

She turns on the radio to drown out her mother rambling about this, that, and the other thing. Her mind begins to drift once again about Diane and the text messages she sent last night. She feels queasy realizing once again, too late, she is not supposed to drink coffee. Little one is protesting and nausea is surfacing. She reaches over to her bag and pulls out a few peanuts from her protein stash.

Her mother, like a hawk, notices something. "What's wrong dear? Why are you eating peanuts at this time in the morning? I remember you usually don't eat anything until almost 10 am and coffee is all you ever want," Sam questions with a flare of accusation.

Sue is too tired and cannot think of a legitimate rebuttal, so she just eats her peanuts in silence, and her nausea readily subsides. Little one …now settles in after she just had a rush and jolt following the flow of caffeine to her little system. The peanuts seem to calm down both of them.

Sue finally responds, "I read in a magazine article, if you eat protein early in the morning it will keep down your carb appetite and help you lose weight," she lies. Of course, her vain mother then insists she needs a good handful of peanuts from Sue, depleting her stash for the trip. She makes a note to buy some on the way home.

Fortunately for Sue, her mother is busy texting Tom, and has very little to say to her. She has tried desperately to put Diane's conversation out of her mind. Oddly enough, she feels a certain yearning to talk to Jorge. Perhaps it is merely the fact that Diane saw him at the Pub last night. She rationalizes that *Diane and Jorge deserve each other. They would keep each other on their toes, and if Diane were with Jorge, in an odd way, it would allow Jorge to get to know his child, if she and Diane hung out. That is a perfect idea;* she will encourage Diane to get together with Jorge. She is too preoccupied for a haughty like Jorge, and most likely, he would cheat on her anyway. *If he cheated on Diane, she would just cheat back…would serve him right.*

Time flies by, and before she knows it, she is pulling up to the Norfolk Carnival Port. Her mother thanks her, and as she gets out of the car, Tom walks up to help her with her luggage. As usual, he looks like he came out of a classic country and western stars magazine. He is about 55 years old, silver grey hair, and a reasonable build. He has on his lizard cowboy boots and Levi jeans. He smiles and his pearly white teeth emit a definitive feeling of insincerity as they exchange cordials. That is fine with Sue, since her reciprocation is just as insincere. Although, she is happy her mother is leaving!

All niceties aside, she is able to pull away and think what she needs now. She is able to feel her stomach growl and she knows it is time to feed the growing child inside. The breaks between eating are getting few- and -far between. She realizes what "a grazing cow" means. That is what she is beginning to feel like. She is probably in her 10th week and the morning sickness is subsiding, replaced with a ferocious appetite.

She is proud of herself for reading up on pregnancy and her investing efforts toward the future of this invisible human entity. It is a bizarre idea. She feels sort of like one of those horror films, with an alien growing in her ... Upon that morbid notion, she could swear she feels an internal objection! She just has an intense imagination.

She pulls into a truck stop close by the harbor, and gets out, with Ginger on her leash, ready to explore after being in the car so many hours. Sue gets out and looks across the pink and purple sky. The sun is rising, there is a slight breeze coming off the water, and crisp air, making her reach inside the car for her jacket. She, once again feels the tiny smooth stone. As if by magic, she vaguely remembers a dream she had before her mother walked in. Again, it was the Indian princess hovering close by a bay inlet, with a smile and a knowing look on her face. Sue remembers trying to see what the Indian Princess was looking at, and only saw the water turn purple and stars fall into the water.

She puts Ginger back in the car, and heads inside to see if they have a fresh breakfast burrito and orange juice. As she enters the store, a trucker looks up as he puts on his seatbelt, and watches a female with a familiar bag go into the store. Joseph feels some pressure in his chest, and wonders, *Could it be? The bag looks the same, and she would be about that age?* ...Is that the same girl he saw before? He starts his truck and as he is leaving the parking lot, he looks over and sees the dog sticking her head out the window. He remembers the girl he had seen a couple of weeks ago. Joseph feels almost like a stalker as he writes down her tag number, feeling like a perpetrator. He quickly turns his head back towards his windshield, just missing Sue's face as she steps out of the store. She gazes out at her dog, and Ginger is barking relentlessly, as if she just missed her long lost owner. Sue chuckles to herself and reaches in the window to pet Ginger. She instinctively looks up long enough to see a purple cab semi leaving the parking lot. She remembers seeing a truck like that before and thoughtlessly rubs the stone in her pocket as she gets into her car, ready to get back to the girls.

Reflections

Joseph runs over the curb, and feels his truck tilt up and over the edge. This is unlike him with the years of truck driving experience he has under his belt. He dares to hope this could possibly be his *Hachi* (Seminole meaning stream). He remembers when he gave her that nickname, when they were skipping rocks in a stream on their last trucking trip together. He wonders if she even remembers that name, he only used it a few times with her on the road trip. He mumbles to himself as he remembers the smooth stones he picked up for both of them. He treated them as if they were magic and told her, when she ever needed him, she should rub her stones. He opens his glove compartment and pulls out a tiny leather pouch. As he stops at a light, he opens the worn bag and pulls out a smooth grey stone about the size of a half dollar. He rubs the stone, and says to himself and the universe at large, "If you are out there and thinking of me, I pray we would find each other." The light changes and he places the rock back in the bag and places it on the seat beside him, keeping an eye on it as if he has just found a secret treasure.

Reflections

He heads back to his office after an all-night run. On the way back, he continues to reflect on his history of long ago. He remembers first meeting Samantha Jones, a beautiful and precocious female working at a local truck stop in Cleveland, Ohio. She was so lovely and very intriguing, as she played hard to get. He would stop by the truck stop in order to catch her eye, and offer a humorous flirtatious comment. He loved their lemon meringue pie and sometimes would eat two pieces and drink an entire pot of coffee. Upon seeing him arrive, Sam would have his pie and coffee sitting at the bar, near where she would deliver her order to Bourbon Black, whose nickname was B.B. because he could drink a quart of Bourbon and his skin was black as night. He was a big, burly man of few words, and when he had his chef's hat on, he ran that crew like a well- oiled wheel. B.B. was an awesome cook, and made a chicken fried steak that any hen would be proud to have named after.

One night, waiting for Sam to finish up her shift, B.B. caught Joseph's attention, giving him a wink, he said in a gruff voice, with a slight chuckle, "Boy, you better watch what you wish for… you might get it… and then not know what to do with it." He took that as a complement and challenge, versus a stern, cynical warning. In hindsight, he should have spent a little more time evaluating that conversation. However, for him, the challenge began at that moment.

Following what seemed to be forever, he finally asked her to go out to the movie with him. They decided to go to the drive in because Joseph wasn't much on dressing up, and he felt comfortable when in a drivers' seat. That was his element. He drove trucks since he could barely reach the petals, and although he was only 21, the last several years felt like an eternity on the road.

Samantha was vivacious and full of aspirations and imaginings of travel and adventure. She said she never wanted children and just wanted to be free and "on the road." He thought she was a match made in heaven. He noticed she would become moody and morose, expressing frustrations when he had to be on the road, and sometimes wanted to quit her job and travel with him. Eventually after six months or so, he picked her up following her late shift. They went out to the harbor, and sitting on the dock, with the moon shining on the shimmering, smooth waves, he pulled out the box. She noticed him putting his hands into his coat pocket, thinking nothing of the gesture since it was nippy as the docks can be in the evening. He turned around slowly, got down on one knee, proposed to Samantha, catching her off guard.

Sammy, as well as being young, full of mischief, hope and dreams, was a very calculating young woman. As quickly as he could ask, she began to evaluate cost versus risk. It wasn't she didn't care for Joseph; it was the fact that Sam primarily cared for herself. That is just her upbringing. "Take care of yourself, because no one else will take care of you." That was the philosophy of her rigid grandmother, Nana, who primarily raised her. Her mother was in and out of her life, but she saw her grandmother as her mother figure, which wasn't saying too much.

Sammy figured she could get out of Cleveland if she married Joseph; after all, he had big ideas of owning his own trucking company. Unfortunately, within the first three months, she was pregnant with Sue. Samantha went from a reasonably nice wife, to a mean as hell bitch. Her moods began to shift and nothing Joseph did was right. By the time, she had the baby, she resented the fact her hopes and dreams of travel dashed. To make things worse, Sue was the apple of Joseph's eye. From the moment he gazed at her and held her close, the bond was invincible.

**

Joseph arrives at his office as some of the other drivers are checking and preparing the trucks for their runs. Joseph is not obligated to drive his truck, he now makes enough money and the business has grown substantially. However, he still enjoys the powerful feeling of being so high in the cab of his truck, as if on top of the world. He loves the roar of the engine and the sense of momentum as he shifts gears. He knows when he is on the road, others around him are attentive to his truck, and his acuity to others around him becomes a philosophy. Unlike many drivers who allow themselves to drive too many hours, and forget their lethal power, indulging in dozing at the wheel, he lives and trains his drivers to remember the safety of others. That way of life is what built his business. Truckers know he will not push them with unreasonable and dangerous time and route expectations. He practices what he preaches and demonstrates consistent caring for the drivers, their wellbeing, and in return, they offer him dedicated reliability.

He checks with his dispatcher, and then pulls out his little leather bag with the stone in it. As he stands day dreaming, Adam, the dispatcher taps him on the shoulder, "Hey Mr. Stark, wanted you to check the progress of these drivers who are running into some serious rainstorms. One of them has an empty load and says his trailer almost jack-knifed.

He is requesting to stop at a truck stop until the rains and hail slow down, but that could be all day based on the weather report."

Joseph appears to be in a malaise, but glances up and says, "Yes, of course, I would rather he arrive alive and late." Grabbing his bag and putting the stone in his pocket, he heads for the house, hoping Jeff has not left for the hospital, yet. He has a deep need for a heart-to-heart talk with an old friend.

CHAPTER 16

John has been beside himself, unable to find Maria, and preoccupied, unable to focus on any of his cases, and his campaign manager shunned. He called Ms. DeBoe several times, only to get the intervention squad of designer groupies she has working for her, to keep him at bay. He feels anxious, agitated, abandoned and afraid, but does not have a clue what he was really feeling. He can only sum his intense emotions as ANGER. With John, if he cannot control it, fix it, or subdue it, he ultimately feels anger. It is not always explosive anger, but often a seething, searing, subtlety, as dangerous as a quiet rattlesnake waiting to strike. This is one of those times; no one really wants to get in his way. He receives a call from the PI who says he found Jorge's vehicle and put the tracker on his truck. He is exhilarated to hear this news and immediately begins to track Jorge's movement from the Pub, he thinks he knows exactly where Jorge is headed… towards Maria's father's store, but then he turns into the parking lot somewhere in the middle of the city. There his truck has not moved. He sent the PI back out to see if he can find Jorge, and when the PI arrives at location, there it is… the device. It is sitting in the middle of the parking lot, looking like a lonely and ineffective tool. The PI stands there feeling a little silly calling Mr. Fisher to tell him he is in the middle of an empty parking lot with a tracking device and no truck.

John has an agitated lonely night with visual ruminations and obsessions about Maria. He wakes up in restless fits, as if he cannot breathe, sweating, and swearing all at the same time. It is the longest night he can remember. His dreams fluctuate from himself being terrified as a child, to seeing Jorge begging him to stop hitting Maria. He can see Maria's petrified eyes, his mother's horrified eyes, and finally awakens begging for forgiveness to whoever will listen. He doesn't have much faith in God. He prayed as a child, and felt his prayers hit the ceiling and bounce back when his father's relentless demands continued despite his begging for celestial interventions. His desperation and helplessness push him to prayers once again, "Lord, you know I can be mean and selfish. You have given me so many things I take for granted.

I am angry and unhappy most of the time, but I ask if you would help me to hear from my wife and know she is safe... AMEN" He suddenly feels calmer. If there is a God, he thinks He will listen to that prayer, mostly because it is one of the first times he admits his faults, doesn't blame anyone else and is not being self-serving. He really does care and wants to find out his wife is safe.

Jorge arrives at the warehouse late because he had an intuition he needed to stop somewhere and look for a tracker on his truck. His father had bragged about his efforts of finding various people who had disappeared with tracking devices and PI's. He noticed the past several days, a particular vehicle seemed to be within the vicinity of just about any place he landed himself. There was the same measly looking man that could have been straight out of the movies. He had on a wrinkled brown sports coat, baseball cap and when Jorge was close enough to see the man, who inevitably had a big cup of 7-11 coffee. He wonders if there must be a manual on dress code and habits of PI's. Jorge takes several diversionary paths and sees the grey old Honda Accord pass by. He did not see him at all last night so he had a creepy feeling he should check and see if there was a tracking device on his truck.

He pulls into the empty parking lot and, voila, there it is. He thinks it most appropriate to leave it right there under the big spotlights. He leaves the lot and picks up pizza, and follows the directions to the warehouse. It is obscure and close by the shoreline, which makes sense based on his mother's new job. Knowing his father's desperation to find her, he worries he may derive a conclusion and start looking out here. He needs to hide his truck realizing the PI will be back on his tail shortly. He finds his mother and she tells him there is a small, empty garage around the corner where he can park his truck.

He feels a little more at ease with his truck out of sight, and realizes how hungry he is as he opens the pizza box and takes a whiff. He bought his mother a chicken Alfredo and himself a supreme. He pulls out the pizzas as well as some sodas and walks into the warehouse. He sees a big metal structure and a couple of hands moving rapidly, pulling various colored cloths around the bracing. He is marveling at his mother's techniques, reminding him of so many projects she had done at home, when he is tapped on the shoulder... startled and ready to punch the PI in the face, he whirls around and sees no one until he looks down. There is his little tiny mother. She laughs at his startled response. She could rarely scare him teasingly as a child, but here as a grown man, she has succeeded! She feels humored and he is confused.

His mother is standing beside him, so whose hands had he admired? Looking a little closer, he notices the hands are not a coffee color, but more of an ivory. Before he can utter a word, his mother is saying, "Sarah, our pizza finally arrived." Sarah mumbles something from behind the metal casing and he can only see a shadowy form until Sarah moves into full view.

She is in sweat pants and a jersey, but fills it out perfectly. He is looking from the floor upwards. First, he sees her white Nikes and her perfectly shaped ass. Her waist, even in athletic clothes looks tiny, especially compared to her bust line. He isn't aware he is holding his breath, but his mother is watching every expression and movement of her son. She can see he is holding his breath and is amused and pleased. Jorge finally gazes into those luscious blue eyes and thinks he could swim in them. Her blonde hair is tight in a ponytail that flings around, as she feels somewhat embarrassed at the look from Jorge.

Sarah, aware she is attractive, has never paid much attention to her looks since her goal since childhood has been to have a career in design. She feels God has graced her with beauty and doesn't have to work at it much. What she enjoys is the work involved in making something beautiful from nothing. Her father is a very handsome man, but very humble, so haughty handsome men never have done much for her. She simply looks at Jorge, glancing at his tight fitting Lucky Jeans, and black leather jacket. Maria introduces them. As beautiful as Sarah appears, Jorge catches himself gawking and realizes he had enough gaming with Diane, shifting his attention to his mother's safety.

The atmosphere shifts as Jorge puts down the pizzas and adoringly puts his mother's face in his hands. "Mi Madre, you must realize my Father, your husband, is relentless and is angry and desperate to find you. I am worried what he will do if he finds you."

Maria kisses her son's hand and says, "Don't worry, I have been married long enough to John and have been planning this for months. I have a Judge who has told me if John even comes near me; he will grant me a VPO. I have known this Judge for years. He is a Hispanic Catholic that went to church with my family when I was growing up. I have a few selfies I have taken the last several times your father hit me. I have testimonies from Ms. DeBoe of how often I have come to work with bruising, and more than anything, the strategic plan of ruining his political career if he comes after me. A server will give him divorce papers tomorrow. Jorge, I love your father, and somewhere in there, years ago, there was a good man. I think he could really help the community if he put his mind to it, but I am done with living in fear. If I do have to move to Mexico, I will. I am going to live my life. God has given me a wonderful son and many talents and I plan to enjoy the rest of my life without abuse."

Sarah feels awkward overhearing this conversation, so she takes her pizza and resumes her work. She begins to feel fatigue, and drops a big drop of pizza sauce on her new white tennis shoes. She says to herself, *Shoot, I shouldn't have worn these new shoes tonight.*

Jorge listens to her mild exclamations, and feels small in character as he realizes had that happened to his new shoes there would have been far more intense and nasty vocabulary erupt from his mouth. He and his mother engage in a little small talk and Sarah walks towards her car parked close by and excuses herself from the evening. Maria recognizes the seriousness of her current situation, and although a little disappointed the moment of light between Sarah and Jorge, squelched rapidly, there will always be opportunities ahead. Despite the sense of sadness related to the death of a long marriage, she has an even greater sense of enthusiasm to engage in her future. She feels lighter, as if a dark cloak is dropping off.

CHAPTER 17

Sue drives the early morning hours with an uneventful trip. The sky glows as the sun comes up over the horizon of the east coast line, and the clouds illuminate purple, pink wisps with feathery white melded throughout. Ginger lies quietly in the back seat, snoring lightly, with an occasional growl or whine depicting a doggie dream and its drama. Sue feels surreal as her thoughts move from internal, feeling the slight butterflies of the unborn child, wondering what may happen inside of her womb; and what the child may experience throughout the day. She is sure the baby has the days and nights mixed up because the night hours bring with it many feelings and sensations she does not experience in the daytime.

Reflections

Sue smiles to herself, thinking, perhaps this child is taking after her. She finds herself remembering how often she would lay there quietly, in her bed, waiting until her little sisters had quit giggling. She would breathe shallow waiting until her mother and stepfather were not fighting, yelling or talking in the other room. Then, getting out of her bed, pulling all of her stuffed animals out from under her bed, she would place them on top of her bed, and talk to each one. She kept them hidden away in the daytime after her mother walked in one day while she was playing with them, and told her, "I am going to throw out those stuffed animals… you are too old to be playing with those. You have two younger sisters you need to help with and you can play with them." She knew intuitively, if she hid the toys under the bed, her mother would forget her words. Sam lived with the concept of out of sight, out of mind, and this would prove to be no exception. Sue recalled her relief each night as she would pull her box out from under her bed and there, once again, her committed family of stuffed animals was awaiting her company.

She named one in particular, "Teddy," and he was her oldest and most favorite teddy bear. Teddy was a cuddly, brown, soft bear, with a pleasant look and sewn in eyes that appeared to be watching her no matter where he sat in the room. Teddy procured a particular musty smell reminding her of the harbor and fishing trips with her father. Joseph had bought it for her when she was a baby, and she could not remember life without Teddy. She believed Teddy brought messages between her and her father after he left. She imagined when she would unzip her bag, hearing him say, "Hurry Sue, hurry."

She would bring him out quickly, smooth his legs down and apologize wholeheartedly, saying, "Sorry Teddy, but we made it." She still had Teddy, who lay carefully on her pillow each morning. She had mended Teddy numerous times throughout her lifetime, and he seems to have fared well, despite multiple transitions and hiding over the years. She committed to herself to give Teddy to the baby, and perhaps it will rekindle her faith in finding her father.

* *

She has felt so helpless over the years to search for her father, she had all but forgotten as an adult, she actually has a choice and her mother cannot stop her, threaten her, or inhibit her from her search. She reaches into her purse to connect with her stones, and for some reason, she thinks once again of the purple semi she had seen twice. She feels a simultaneous fleeting thought, and movement, when she pictures the truck driver in her mind. She wonders, *but no, that driver was too young to be my father, wasn't he?* About that moment, she feels a wet nuzzle on her neck and dog breath arriving at her nostrils, with an automatic, "Yuck, Ginger, your breath is terrible... no don't lick me..." Ginger whines and she decides she is going to have to stop one more time before she arrives back at her mother's home.

She nibbles on trail mix, some peanut butter crackers, and gives Ginger several doggie snacks, but her tummy begins to demand more sustenance. She feels odd, craving a pickle, and butter pecan ice cream. She doesn't even like pickles. She has heard rumors about cravings but believes women most likely just use cravings as an excuse to eat more what they love. Now she craves pickles and ice cream in the morning? Who would have thought of this combination? She is going to stop and indulge herself and the baby, but needs to look up on Google some answers to these cravings.

She is about 5 miles from Dale City, on I -95. She sees a sign for Quales Truck stop featuring BarBQ. She is confident... *where there is BarBQ, there are pickles. It is crazy*; she can visualize herself biting into one of those giant pickles found in one of those giant jars, with the milky green water and garlic pods floating around. Instead of disgust, she actually feels her palate begin to water. *How weird.* With the mere thought of adding any sort of ingestion of food, somehow, her bladder is cued and suddenly she has to pee so badly. She pulls in with the pumps on the right, and several trucks in front of the station. She has a sense of kinship with the truck stop. It brings her closer to her father. Ginger is wagging her tail, and nervously pacing the back seat, ready to exit. Sue checks out the grass behind the store with plenty of room for Ginger to do her business. She has to tell Ginger to wait, with her bladder feeling it is about to explode. Ginger whines, but seems to understand, as she plops back down with a grunt.

Without being too conspicuous, Sue hurries inside, scanning the walls for a sign for the restrooms. As she glances up, her keen senses spot a large pickle jar by the BarBQ area, and she notes her first craving will soon be satisfied. With relief, she spots the bathroom sign and heads for the women's, and bypasses the shower room. She finds it amusing to see the machines for condoms and Kotex. She feels regret that she had not been smart enough to stop at a truck stop before her rendezvous with Jorge. The sensation she experiences with her negative regretful thoughts are very noticeable now. She used to think they were just her imagination; however, with each week of gestation, the sensation seems to be more intense and distinctive. Meanwhile, *little one* has enjoyed being well cared for and acknowledged. This most recent thought/feeling of her mother created a huge disturbance of uncertainty.

Once she and Ginger relieve their bladders and both eat some food, she settles in for the last portion of her trip back to her mother's home. Her mind wanders aimlessly moving from memories of her father and wondering what he may be like after so many years, and if he ever thinks about her, to pondering why Diane was in contact with Jorge, and why she had met with the perverted manager. Her instinct is bothering her, but as she has done so often in her life, she feels herself trying to ignore the feeling that Diane may not be out for her best interest. An internal, audible voice saying, *Trust your instinct.* Therefore, she decides to call into the office and get a little feedback from her *loyals.*

Jennifer answers the phone, "Your favorite team member waiting on marching orders."

Sue laughs and asks, "How is your chief, Diane doing in my spot?"

Jenn changes the subject and asks Sue how the trip has been so far. Jenn doesn't want Sue to worry but has noticed Diane snooping around in files she probably shouldn't be in. Sue tracks back to the original question but words it differently, "Is Diane sticking to what she is supposed to be doing?" She feels some guilt for asking, but cannot stop the feeling that something is awry with Diane.

Jennifer fesses up, "I think she has been going through some of the management files and team building files."

Someone could have hit Sue right between the eyes. She feels almost sick as she thinks to herself, *could she be setting herself in a position to take my job? After all, she knows I'm pregnant. What if she tells my senior manager I do, and offers to work at a lower commission?* She is not responding to Jennifer, and there is some lengthy silence on the phone.

Jennifer is regretful she said anything. "Hey Sue, I shouldn't have said that. I am sure it is nothing. We miss you…and will be glad when you get back." Silence….

Sue realizes she has not said anything since the disclosure about Diane. She responds to Jennifer, trying to be upbeat and cautious at the same time, "Well, I probably *am indispensable*, so be my eyes and ears. I know I can trust you to note anything unusual that I may need to know. Just call if you need to… There is a little technicality of new promotions, etc.," and Sue hangs up feeling extremely anxious.

Jennifer goes into the bathroom, and on the john, she begins to pray, "God, if there is something I need to know, show me. Sue is a good manager and she seems like she is going through a rough time… Please help her. In Jesus' name," she mumbles. As soon as she flushes the toilet, she sees some extremely high heels under the door in the next stall and knows immediately it is Diane. *She is the only one that dresses like she is going to a night club, when she is merely sitting at a desk most of the day.*

Jenn takes her time washing her hands, as she puts on a little lipstick and pulls her hair back in a ponytail. Diane comes out of the stall with her cell phone in her hand, preoccupied, texting. Diane looks up in the mirror as if it were a magnet calling her to look into it to affirm her beauty. She is slow to recognize there is another face gazing at her and reacts startled. Jenn is amused at the entire scene of a woman she perceives is extremely self-centered, and is concerned about what that self-centeredness may connive.

As often as Sue has avoided any favors from Jack, she knows he respects her work as well as her independence. Little does she realize, he actually admires her consistent dismissal of his sexual advances? If the truth is told, he rarely goes through with any sexual acts with his subordinates. He unwittingly uses this as a sort of test to determine if someone wants to merely climb the ladder through spreading their legs versus the work ethic he believes is required to make it into management level.

Sue spends the next hour or so ruminating and obsessing about what may be happening at the office. She finally decides to dial Jack's number, when her cell phone rings. It is Sarah, her sister, calling to ask Sue her ETA and if she could pick them up some lunch. She is about an hour from her mother's home. Sarah chatters about the plans for the weekend, and all the activities she and Sylvia have in store for her. She can hear Sylvia in the background, asking to have Sue pick up some Subway, but Sarah wants pizza. Sue finds herself laughing and deciding she will placate both of them and stop by a pizza shop that carries subs, also.

She stops to get gas, and while she is pumping the gas, she gets on her phone and Googles pizza and subs off I 95, Baltimore, MD. She is in luck; there is Jerry's Pizza and Subs off I 95. She calls in an order and says she will be there in about 40 min. Her stomach growls and she feels some fluttering movement. She smiles down and pats her tummy…"O.K. O.K… you cannot wait an hour to eat?" Ginger wines and she almost forgot she is back there. "Alright, I will take you potty and get you a doggie snack!!! Geez, the survival needs have kicked in!" She gathers her purse and hooks on Gingers leash, leaving her phone charging in the car. She exits and stretches, taking Ginger to a small area of green grass. She misses the call from the unknown number.

Meanwhile, Jorge thought perhaps if he calls from an unknown number, Sue might just answer. He lets it ring until her voicemail states, "This person is not taking calls at this time, please try back later." He cusses to himself, and has to get back to the bank, after his 15-minute break. He breaths in and exhales slowly. Sometimes he can be impatient, but when there is a challenge, he merely develops alternative strategies.

CHAPTER 18

Sue mindlessly listens to Siri tell her every turn, number of miles, exit markers, etc. until she arrives at Jerry's Pizza and Sub shop. Entering the parking lot at the address of the sub shop, Sue reassures Ginger she will be back shortly to take her potty. She walks in, the smells of pizza dough and pepperoni hit her nostrils, and she has a blend of hunger and nausea. She has been fairly nausea free, but there is something else in the air. Only certain things now cause her queasiness and one of them is cheap male cologne. Standing on the other side of the room, is a male in his 30's, with a red plaid, cowboy shirt, dirty, muddy black boots, black wrangler jeans, and messy hair. She cannot see his face, but she can smell his cologne and it overpowers her. She turns pale white and before she can pick up her order, she is ready to abort her food mission and just exit, when the young man's phone rings and he walks outside, with the unpleasant odor following him. The owner of the shop is observing Sue and is about to ask her if she needs some help, but watches her transform from a friendly, flushed-face attractive female, to a pale white, distressed and desperate woman. Here she is again, the pleasant looking female. *What had just happened?*

He approaches her from across the counter. He hesitantly asks, "Ma'am, can I help you, you look rather ill or upset, it is difficult to tell?" She is intensively watching to see if the other male is going to re-enter. She is unaware of any particulars about the man behind the counter, but answers and questions at the same time, never letting her eyes leave the door. "I have an order to pick up, but I think I am allergic to the smell of that guy outside...do you think he is coming back in? If he does, I will have to leave. I promised myself I would not get sick while I am in Maryland." Sue is as serious as she can be, and the man behind the counter bursts out laughing.

"You and many others are allergic to Jester's cheap smelling cologne. He comes in everyday to shoot the bull and then leaves after having a sub sandwich. He swears he is the next Jared Fogle, negating the sexual exploits, and has lost about 45lbs eating our subs. He is leaving

He has to be back to work at his father's cattle ranch." She breathes a sigh of relief, and finally turns around to look up at the counter and see the face of the man who just helped to quell her fears of hugging the toilet. She notices a gentle, face with nice laugh lines. His eyes are brown, with nice brows, a firm chin, and a great laugh. She thinks he is most likely about 28 years old, maybe a little older. She instinctively notices his left hand does not have a ring, and then scolds herself internally for even allowing such a thought to cross her mind.

She feels some movement and remembers reading about mothering instincts, and if a woman does not have a father for the baby, she will begin to pursue it as a natural survival mechanism. She feels very impressed her natural mothering disposition is intruding upon her usual reserved self, and wants to observe this new character quality without resistance... *Why not? It will be harmless*, she is far from home and she seldom lets herself be reckless. On second thought, the last time she was reckless, she ended up with a baby in utero. Perhaps this is not a good idea. She smiles cautiously, and says, "I would have paid you, even if I had to leave without the order."

He shakes his head, humored all the more by her response. "Oh, you would have, huh? Well, if you didn't, I don't think I would have called the police and ran out to get your license plate."

He wipes his hands off on his apron and introduces himself as "Jerry."

She says, "As in Jerry the owner?"

"Yes, as in Jerry the owner."

Sue feels a little spark of sensation as she shakes his hand, and pulls her hand away quickly and moves her fingertips through her hair, brushing it behind her ears. "Oh, I am sorry for taking so much time. I know you must be terribly busy and I need to get my order and head out. I have a couple of younger sisters who are most likely in some sort of battle since I should have been to their home about now," says Sue.

Jerry pulls out a bag and says, "You must be Sue?" Sue turns red again as she is amazed he knows her name.

As if he read her mind, Jerry says, "That is the name you made the order for, and since we have no other to go orders, I assumed you are Sue?"

Sue clears her throat and says, "Yes, that is me…How much do I owe you?"

Jerry ponders Sue's fluctuation between engaging and disengaging. He says, "Well, since Jester's smell almost made you ill, I will let this order be on me." He continues, "On one condition, if you are staying anywhere within a 60-mile radius, and unmarried and not engaged or in a serious relationship, I would love to take you out."

By this time, Sue is sipping a straw in the 7Up she purchased, and almost spits it out as she chokes and the fizz goes up her nose. Jerry laughs again. "Wow, I hope you are not insulted I asked you out?" Before she could answer, he hands her a card and says, "Give me a call if you get bored while in Maryland. I could meet you somewhere so you don't think I am some sort of serial killer. I just happen to know when an opportunity is looking me in the face, and you are definitely a fun opportunity."

Sue isn't quite sure what he means by opportunity, but she takes his card and slips it into her wallet. She tries one more time to pay, but he just hands her the bag and tells her to enjoy.

Sue hops into the car and checks her rear view mirror, only to see a big slobbery tongue and mouth panting with the sound of intermittent whining. She is startled, having been preoccupied with the last interaction. "I am so sorry girl, I forgot all about you. I am surprised I do not have a big wet spot in the seat." She gets a gut feeling, looks a little closer, and sees that Ginger had indeed not been able to hold it…. "Oh no, I cannot live with the smell of dog pee all the way home!!!!" she sighs exasperated. "First things first… I better take you out before you take a dump, also," Sue says in an aggravated tone.

Ginger lies down on the seat and puts her paws over her head, as if to say, "Don't be mad at me."

Sue feels disjointed because it is not Ginger's fault, but now she must drive with the smell of urine all the way either home, or muster up the courage to go back in and face Jerry. That entire scene was awkward, and now she has to re-engage with the man. It would be one thing if she left, had a day or two to reflect, and then perhaps give him a call….or not? Now, she has to walk back in there. She puts Ginger's leash on her and takes her towards the back of the shop. Fortunately, her car is parked on the side, and is not visible from the counter. She lets Ginger sniff around and she too aimlessly rambles among the tall weeds and considers what she can do. Sue remembers seeing the bathrooms to the right when you first enter the shop. She thinks she can sneak in, veer to the right, and if she's in luck, he will be behind the counter cooking or something. She can grab some paper towels, put some soap on a few wet ones, and soak most of it up, leaving it soapy, but at least it won't smell like urine.

Ginger has long since done her business and is merely walking around and sniffing. Sue feels her tugging on the leash and is brought back into the moment. She feels a surge of confidence and puts Ginger in the car, pulls back her shoulders, throws her hair to the back of her neck and walks up to the door. Her courage leaves quickly as she glances at the counter and does not see anyone. Well, that could be her opportunity. She scurries through the door, hangs right, moves past the first yellow booth, and is able to push through the bathroom door without being seen. She grabs the paper towels, and then has the physical urgency to go to the bathroom herself… *So much for a quick get-a-way… Little one is already so demanding…* She stops midway through pulling down multiple sheets of paper towels, places them on the edge of the sink and goes inside one of the stalls. She hears the door open, but it doesn't close. She tries to look underneath the stall towards the door, but doesn't see anyone. She pulls up her panties and sweat pants, starts to flush the toilet, and about that time, notices a mop gliding over the outer rim of her stall. She freezes, and then sees some tennis shoes that seem excessively big to be lady's shoes. They are New Balance and those can look the same… She reassures herself and flushes the toilet.

She then distinctly hears a man's voice saying, "I am so sorry, and I had on my ear buds and did not realize anyone was in here. Please excuse me."

Sue doesn't say anything, but can feel her heartbeat and respiration racing. She hears the door close and stays in the stall for a few moments. She notices the paper towels she had pulled down, are in the trash, so she pulls some more down, dampens one and puts soap on it. She calms down and rationalizes, whoever that was, is now tending to other business. She opens the door and notices it is very squeaky, so she slowly creeps around the corner, only to have someone come out of the men's bathroom and come up behind her. She whirls around like a caught criminal, paper towels crumbled and flowing out of both hands.

There stands Jerry, with a huge grin of curiosity on his face. His eyes twinkling, he doesn't have to say a word, before her defenses come gushing out like Niagara Falls. She sounds like she has just been tortured and is giving up her true confessions of a heinous crime. She rambles in rapid, manic-like speech. "You see, I got to my car and my dog had peed all over, so I had to take her back out so she wouldn't take a dump in the car, also. Then I thought I could borrow some paper towels from in here, but because I am pregnant, I had to urgently pee myself, so that is why I was in the stall and all of the paper towels were on the sink counter." She barely had room for a breath during her dialogue, and his look went from amused to concerned as well as confused.

"Slow down Sue… I thought perhaps you reconsidered and were mounting up courage to come back and see me, and that is why you were in the stall. I had no idea you were married and pregnant. Please forgive me for being so overt in my date proposition earlier. Now, how can I help you clean up your mess in the car?" says Jerry.

She is confused at his comments. Did she say anything about being married? *O.K., stands to reason he would assume that. How stupid was that for me to say I am pregnant.* She admonishes herself harshly… *Why did you have to bring that up? He did not need to know that information. The only person that even knows about the pregnancy is Diane, and it isn't looking like she is very trustworthy… Now, the person you just met knows your secret.* She is unsure how long she stands there, but she can tell Jerry is nervous and uncertain about what he needs to do next.

He clears his throat, shuffles his feet, looks down, and then gazes upwards nervously. She says, "I am not married, or engaged, but had some unfortunate judgment with the wrong kind of person." His face changes immediately. He doesn't know whether to be happy or run the other direction from an obviously fickle woman. In not knowing what to do, he does the first thing that comes to mind, he turns around and goes back into the men's restroom and grabs some towels and Orange Plus, earth friendly cleaning products. By the time he turns around the corner of the bathroom, he can see Sue's back headed out the door. *What was he thinking, to completely turn his back to her and re-enter the men's bathroom? What must Sue have felt?*

He attempts to rush out the door, but the floor is wet, so he looks like Scooby Doo, with legs moving and going nowhere.

Meanwhile, Sue grumbles to herself, *how humiliating! He turned back into the men's bathroom. That brings the idea of "I really don't give a shit" to an entirely literal meaning!* She rationalizes quickly, *oh well, one more complexity I don't need.* As she shuts her door, she hears Ginger sigh. "Oh, don't give me that, you didn't try to warn me, she says to the dog with a short tempered voice." As she backs her car out of the parking lot, she sees Jerry in her rear view mirror, waving his arms like a mad man, holding something in his hands. *What is that?* She takes a whiff of air and smells the strong smell of drying urine, and remembers why she went back in the first place. As she inquisitively looks more closely at what Jerry has in his hand, she takes a second look. Is he waving a cleaning product…. *Can this interaction become any more awkward bizarre?*

Without much thought, she pulls up beside him, pushes her window button, looks in the mirror and adds a touch of lipstick. *This should be good;* she tells herself sarcastically.

He pushes the gallon bottle of Orange Plus in front of him, almost through her window. He stammers, "I went back in to get this to help clean the mess and clear up the odor. It really is a great product."

Sue says, "Are you up for some commission if you sell me on this product?" The ice is broken and both smile, relieved they have past the last conversation. She indirectly accepts his offer by getting out of the car, opening the back door, and letting Ginger out while introducing them. "Ginger, this is Jerry. Jerry, this is Ginger." She gives a small growl and then wags her tail. Jerry muses to himself, *Wow, dog is like her owner…growls and then wags her tail.*

Almost hearing his thoughts, Sue says, "Ginger can sometimes give mixed messages. I guess I have done a pretty good job of that myself?"

"Well, I suppose one congruent thought is, I am standing here with some towels and a great cleaning product, that I am absolutely sure you will both want and need at this moment, to get that horrific smell out of your car. Is that true?" Ginger looks offended, and turns her back on Jerry, watching and barking at a cat crossing the parking lot. Before Sue can grab her leash, Ginger is off in a mad dash to get the cat. The cat, with a good head start, scurries to the other end of the parking lot, where there is a house lot, with several very tall white ash trees, offering refuge as the cat scurries up the tree, with Ginger fast on her tail. Sue is running, walking as she realizes the cat has found safety and Ginger is pre-occupied at the base of the tree. Wow, Sue realizes she has not gone running in almost a month, and she feels weak, with shortness of breath. She has worked so hard at staying fit and trim, only to see it go down the tube in a little over a month. Hands on her hips, she leans over to catch her breath, and while she is leaning over, she feels a hand on her shoulder and jerks around, as Jerry doesn't budge from his comforting stance, realizing how his last exchange most likely felt very rejecting. He thinks, no matter what the outcome of this interaction, he does not want Sue to feel judged or rejected. He can feel the pulse in his hand, as he gently rubs her shoulder.

Sue feels unusually aware of his touch, not exactly electrical, but some warm vibrations of sensuality. She closes her eyes, and breathes in this new sensation. Sue allows Jerry's hand to rest on her shoulder while she gradually regains both composure and steady breath. She gazes up the tree, and is amazed at its height, and the width of the trunk. She moves gracefully walking around the circumference of the tree, with a silent awe at the magnificence of the tree. Jerry walks at a distance, recognizing some depth of character in this fascinating woman he didn't know 2 hours ago, but who seems to have imprinted a significant impression into his mind. She reminds him of cloud formations that move and shift, consistently changing, and always intriguing. Ginger is pleased to have visitors come on her cat chase, so she happily jumps, barks, and tangles both of them up in her leash. Before they know it, they are grabbing her leash and end up tripping and falling on the ground. Ginger licks both of them, as they attempt to untangle themselves. Jerry says, "Well, at least I was smart enough to put the towels and cleaning product down by the car. That would have added some fun with cleaning solution all over us."

He leans over her lap to unwind the leash from around her waist. She smells Jerry and he definitely does not smell like cheap cologne. He smells like a delicious combination of fresh baked bread, and what was the name of that cologne she smelled last time she was in Macy's?... the one she thought about buying Jorge when they were a "thing," or at least that is what she thought. Let's see, the name was something like, "Sexy Sugar Daddy." She mumbles the last to herself, but slightly aloud.

He chuckles, what do you mean by, "Sexy Sugar Daddy?" She did not realize she had said that where he could hear.

Once again, she begins to ramble, "Well, you smell good, like bread and some cologne I remember and it was called "Sexy Sugar Daddy?"

He chuckles, "You mean, Michel Germain... Sexy Sugar Daddy?"

She feels her phone vibrating, and realizes she put her phone on silent. Sue mindlessly answers and hears both sisters upset, with loud voices, "Where are you? We have been expecting you for over an hour. We are starving. Have you picked up our food? When are you gonna be here?" The phone is on speaker and Jerry can hear their distress, realizing the pizza and subs are far from hot and unsure how long all of these dynamics have been transpiring. He feels relieved his second shift person is due at noon, and is most likely covering the noon rush. He reluctantly realizes he needs to head back, and feels like a balloon with a leak, deflating quickly. He is unsure if he will ever see this unique woman again, but regardless, has responsibilities beckoning him back.

Sue gets up off the ground and dusts herself off, takes her hair tie off her wrist, and then tosses her hair forward and pulls her hair up into a ponytail. Since taking prenatal vitamins, her hair has thickened and lengthened. Jerry, despite his sudden sense of anxious urgency, takes in a deep gaze, as if her movement was in slow motion, her hair flying around like a horse's mane in the wind, and then tied down and constricted. He gulps as he feels his groin likewise constricting. Annoyed at his physical reactions without his willful control, he focuses on his responsibilities. He realizes he needs to speed it up as he looks at his watch and it says it is 12:30pm. *Where did time fly?* He left his phone on the counter and he is sure Tommy is wondering where he disappeared to... This is unlike his usual dependability... Several years have gone by since emotionally connecting to a female.

Reflections

A little over two years ago, he somehow managed to get out of an extremely chaotic relationship. His girlfriend, Shanna, was like Dr. Jekyll and Mr. Hyde in her personality. She was so diligent and determined to set goals, like finishing her Associates degree in Recreational Therapy in less than 2 years. She was smart, sweet and beautiful until... something did not go her way, or he could not be available for her needs.

Then… she would become aggressive and hateful. She was like a sleek panther, beautiful and dangerous. He tried to please her, until it began to hurt his self-image. Nothing he could do was good enough, fast enough, or right in her eyes. He found himself being micro managed and second-guessing himself in all of his endeavors.

He was finally able to put away some money from bartending in the city, as well as from the inheritance he received when his grandmother passed away. He had to make a decision. Shanna was pushing him to get her a huge engagement ring and plan for a very costly wedding. His grandmother had been an amazing cook, and according to stories, she had a restaurant in her earlier years that had been quite successful. He saw the sub shop for sale, and felt a sense of sentimentality about using his grandmother's money to buy it. Shanna gave him an ultimatum, either her or the sub shop, and he decided on the sub shop.

Now, as simple as that decision may seem, she was a fighter. She would not let him go. She harassed him, texting 20-30 times a day, calling incessantly, putting nasty messages on face book, and ultimately, turning friends against him. He almost caved, but fortunately, the price of the sub shop reduced in price by $10,000. He was sure it was an omen from the heavens… He could almost hear, "Run Forest, run." So, despite the pain, the rages, the begging and pleading, he set his course. Shanna had a lot of charm and influence, so she was able to gain the allegiance of most of his friends, and even a few of his family members were watching and waiting for him to "eat crow," with regrets of losing Ms. Shanna.

No such devastation occurred, instead, he dug his heels in, began a significant amount of research in marketing a sub shop, determining to add pizza, using the past down recipe of his grandmother. He built an amazing pizza oven that had brought some local notoriety. He worked long, hard hours, and was fortunate to hire Tommy, who was a godsend. Even this very moment, he knew he could depend on levelheaded Tommy, who worked steady, had a pleasant, unwavering disposition, with a slight edge of dry humor to keep a little laughter in the environment.

His faith in life, and hope for the future, helped Jerry during the very dark and lonely times following his breakup. He had often thought, if he were the least bit gay, he would have picked a partner like Tommy. Unfortunately, his groin only reacts for females, and then he never knows exactly when it will take on a mind of its own.

**

Jerry holds his hand out, and Sue looks into his eyes, feeling a warmth and friendliness. She chooses to ignore the moisture, and tingling she feels between her legs, almost making her knees buckle. She chalks it up to hormones and pregnancy. She read that sexual drive increases around the second trimester of pregnancy. He almost drags her and Ginger back to her car, and without asking, grabs the cleaning supply and towels and holds out his hands. Without words, she hands him her keys. He opens the backdoor and the smell of urine has blended with the sunny day, causing it to seem caustic. He begins to work like a pro, and before Sue can offer any suggestions, the car begins to smell like fresh oranges, and the color on the seats seems to regain the ivory beige rather than one big brown spot. She whistles, expressing her feelings of being impressed. He chuckles and turns around. "I haven't heard anyone whistle like that since I worked as a bartender and Jake, one of the owners, would exploit his position and whistle at the women as they would walk out."

He smiles and immediately begins to jog around the corner towards the shop. She feels bewildered, and ready to cuss herself under her breath for flirtatious and giddy feelings, when he looks back and says, "Be right back, stay right there."

Now, she is at a loss. Her pizza and subs are getting colder by the minute, her sisters will be put out with her, and now he wants her to wait? Ginger looks up, now settled back in the back seat, curled away from the wet spot near the passenger's door. "I know, we have been here too long, and we need to get on the road. We don't want to hit afternoon traffic, since it is already past 1:00 pm."

She gets into the driver's seat, buckles her seat belt, fixes the mirror and notices her face is looking fuller, and a little pinker than normal. She remembers hearing about the glow of pregnancy, and wonders if it is a man's way of avoiding saying, your face has gotten as round as the moon? Sue wonders what she will look like when she is full term pregnant and has an image of a beached whale, and a sort of disgust floods over her. At that moment, *little one*, highly protesting this negativity, tries her hardest to create movement in her watery home. She is still small enough to turn full circles. She flips repeatedly several times. Sue has learned these cues are some sign of internal protest, and once again, she repents, puts her hand on her belly and says, "I am sorry I said that *little one*. I know my changes are just a part of making room for you and preparing you to come into this world healthy and happy. We will get a jogging stroller and make sure I get my girly figure back, and you enjoy the great park I run at. Help you to love the outdoors, like me… and …" she sadly thinks of her father.

She sits there pondering, unsure of how long she has been sitting, when looking up, she sees a white bag looking her in the face, while Ginger begins to whine and wags her tail. She smells the delicious aroma of fresh pizza, and as she reaches up to bring the bag into her window, she sees it is sitting on a pizza box, held up by Jerry's hand. Sue says, "How much do I owe you for this fresh order?"

Jerry states, "Just reach over into the other seat and hand me the cold ones, and I will take them off your hands. That should do just fine." She inadvertently touches fingers with Jerry and feels the nice tingly sensation. She smiles and catches his boyish grin. "You better head out or you are going to have some angry, hungry sisters, from what I overheard." She feels defensive for just a moment, and then the choice to give it a rest. She realizes she is consistently in a defensive posture. It feels nice just to be playful, without feeling defensive. She trades the pizza boxes and bags, and waves to him as she heads out. Ginger is quietly chewing on a rawhide bone Jerry had given to her right before she pulled out. They are back on the road again. She has the feeling her life has changed, but is unsure what may come of this adventure. Instead of worrying what ought to be, she just allows herself "to be." It feels good, and the *little one* twirls around inside.

CHAPTER 19

Joseph has been disturbed all day. He sits at his desk and vivid memories come flooding into his mind. He remembers… his night was restless with disturbing dreams. He saw her again, the daunting shadowy figure. She wisps past him with deep dark brown eyes, hair flowing. This time is different, she is fearful, fighting; there is blood on her hands. She moves through the darkness, with heavy brush and trees, she seems to be captured, twirling around, then darkness. As if the darkness begins to take form, it becomes a bear, proud and majestic, while fierce at the same moment. Joseph awakens in a cold sweat, unsure what to make of this dream. With the habituation of an insomniac, he robotically gets out of bed, slips on his slippers, turns on his nightlight, and sits on the edge of his bed.

As if the world is in slow motion, he observes the beams of moonlight entering his room. His taste buds flow with a bitter taste and his ears are ringing a deep resonating low note, like the low rumble of the motor in his truck. Rather than reaching for the remote and turning on the T.V. to some late night show, he takes a few deep breaths, getting past the feeling of panic. As if some voice is speaking to his soul, he hears, "Look up your dream." Strange, as enduring and frequent these disturbing dreams have been he never thought to look them up. He isn't exactly sure but he figures he can Google, "Dream meaning." Sure enough, several web pages pop up. Under dreamhawk.com, he reads, "Blood on hands-you have killed or injured some part of yourself." A bear can mean "Courage, maternal nurturing, or protection, but can also represent dealing with a relationship with someone who is powerful."

Reflections

The emotions begin to flood his thoughts and a myriad of precipices come to his mind. He has avoided the helpless feeling of abandoning his daughter all of these years. He knew Samantha was a calculating and vengeful woman. When they had met when he was 21 years old, during their dating period, one of the times he had been on the road for a lengthy period, he had made a fatal mistake. He traveled in rural areas and would often stay at sleazy hotels. She had been playing extra hard to get, and he had been unable to have sex with her for over a month. One night, after he had spoken to Samantha on the phone, she told him she had been considering going out with another local named Quinton, who looked more promising and was out of town less frequently. He was trying to argue his cause, when she said she had to go, someone else was calling. She would not answer the phone again that night.

He remembers that night vividly. He had been driving since early morning, and it was already 10pm. He knew he would be too tired to drive all the way back to Cleveland and that was when he called Sam hoping she would be happy to hear from him and talk him into coming back home; instead he fell short receiving merely manipulation. Aching all over from the long drive, he thought he might as well hunker down for the night. He came up over a winding hill and saw the familiar florescent multicolored lights saying, "VACANCY." He pulled in and noticed the motel and a bar right across the street.

Being of age, he went and bought himself a few shots of Bourbon to drown out his frustration. He was a red blooded American Indian, and the spirit water left him feeling more agitated than ever. As he went back to his hotel, he had the sense to place his gun on his nightstand and empty the cartridges. Apparently, a local pimp while leaving the bar spotted him. Soon he heard some knocking at the hotel room door. He opened the door and an attractive female, with blonde cropped hair, white skirt barely covering her ass, and a pink chiffon, low cut blouse, with pink lips matching, obviously a prostitute, was standing there. She asked if she could come in for a few minutes because her ride had left her. He tried to say no and resist her entrance, but the menacing brew was wreaking havoc on his balance, and she easily pushed her way in. She immediately noticed his wallet sitting on the nightstand, and walked over saying she would pull a trick for $50.00. At this point, he knew he was in a precarious situation. He grabbed her by the arm and moved her towards the door, when another female entered and said they would both do him for $75.00.

The other female, larger in size and intimidating, looked towards the gun and started moving that direction, his instinct made him reach over for the gun. Apparently, the first prostitute had made her contact and the police entered as soon as Joseph had lifted the gun. The females collaborated, stating Joseph had held them at gunpoint and tried to force them for sex. He landed in jail, and had one phone call, and that was to Samantha. He told his woeful story and she sounded comforting, but resulted in nothing more than sitting in jail for over two weeks.

He had no money for an attorney, but based on several other poor schmucks in jail, this was part of this redneck town's funding. Fortunately, his friend Jeff came from an affluent family, and after he hadn't heard from Joseph in over two weeks, he contacted Samantha, who told him where he was located. His father, an attorney, made a few phone calls, and apparently got enough evidence against the police force in that community for numerous cases of malicious prosecution. Joseph was finally released, but not without accruing some criminal history. With a plea bargain though still a felony, he had no more jail time and probation for 10 years. Jeff's father agreed to not let this get out, and Joseph went home weary, shame based, and humiliated.

Samantha had acted very supportive of him when he came home, and seemed all the more committed, leading him to feel obligated, especially since she knew his secret. She mentioned it every so often, during their courtship, but after they had Sue, her comments became more vicious and condescending. Like, "How could I have been so stupid to have married a felon?"

The last time he was with Sue, they were having so much fun on their fishing trip, he did not bring Sue home on the fourth day, but, they decided to stay another night. When Joseph called Sam, she was furious and said she notified the police that he had kidnapped Sue. Every fear imaginable went through his mind as he thought he would go to prison for violating his probation. She told him, if he brought Sue back, she would file for divorce and drop the charges, but if he ever came back into her life, she would say he was abusive and he would go to prison.

Reflecting back, he realizes those threats most likely would not have stood up in court, but at the time, he was still young and had traumatic memories of those two weeks in jail. He didn't see the sun for the entire two weeks, ate green baloney, slept by a leaky toilet with no mattress and his blanket on the floor. There were so many people in the cells, he was fearful for his life. He had no shower, and he smelled like a pig when finally allowed out of his orange suit. He changed jumpsuits one time in the entire two weeks, and was afraid of one of the big ole boys using him as a personal penis plug if he tried to change or shower. He finally changed once in the middle of the night when everyone was asleep.

When Sam gave him that ultimatum, by that time, he knew her vicious disposition, and did not doubt for a minute she would carry out her menacing plan if he crossed her path. Now, he felt so much remorse and regret realizing he had left Sue with such a woman. He pondered what a young girl, who would now be in her early 20's, would think of such an abandoning father. Knowing Sam, he felt sure she would have pumped Sue with toxic malice regarding him, and most likely gave her some terrible story about his character. Even telling the truth would sound bad. For a brief second he considered hiring a private detective to help him locate Sue; however, the voice of shame resonated in his ears. The whispers of self-condemnation at its best, *how could you leave your daughter, your only child, with such a wicked woman? You know she hates you and wishes you were dead. She has most likely vowed to herself never to speak to you, even if you try to find her. You need to just realize how selfish you were.*

**

Saved by a phone call, but he knows deep within his being, the voice will be back. It always is. It torments him day and night, when he sees the Indian woman in his dreams. She looks forlorn, with expressions of the deepest sort of betrayal. He is unsure where she comes from. Is she an ancestral curse? He heard stories how spirits from generations past visit and torment souls until sin is rectified. Whether the folklore is his Native American or Christian church upbringing, it is all similar. I Christianity, it says, "The sins of the fathers are passed down 3 and 4 generations." Joseph considers this possibility of being haunted for the rest of his life by this aberration, and has a deep feeling of helplessness and hopelessness. His energy from the day feels void, and cluttered. Rescued from his thoughts, his phone rings and he hears the chipper voice on the other end, and realizes it is Jeff. He is reminding him of the dinner party tonight at the house, and he needs to pick up a few sirloins on his home from the office.

Joseph finishes the paperwork, invoices, review of routes and drivers, and finally is able to generate some sense of accomplishment and a glimmer of pride in his work.

Reflections

He remembers the day when he wondered if he would ever be able to move beyond his feelings of failure. He was a football player in high school, and grades good despite living in a single parent household. His father left home when he and his brother were still in elementary school. His brother, Ezekiel, was two years older than Joseph. They were like two peas in a pod. Their mother raised them in a unique combination of Christian and Seminole culture.

His grandmother and great grandmother held onto many of the tribal traditions. During their teenage years, their mother attended a Christian Pow Wow, and rather than merely believing in the Great Spirit, she named it the "holy spirit." His grandmother referred to the Creator, but his mother said, "Jesus is the first born of All Creation." It wasn't too hard for Joseph to agree with both, and in his prayers as a child; he would say, "Dear Creator Jesus, and Spirit of holiness…" It made him feel good, and he thought, despite his father leaving, he had a Father in Heaven… until the terrible day… His brother had been showing a friend their father's gun, and didn't know it had a bullet lodged in the chamber. The gun slipped. Ezekiel shot himself in the head. When the ambulance arrived, he was dead. When Joseph came home, the gurney holding his brother's dead body w a s covered with a sheet. He recalled jumping out of the car of one of the neighbors and running as fast as he could before the ambulance closed the doors. He pushed and shoved the EMTs until they agreed to let him remove the sheet and say goodbye.

He fell on top of Ezekiel, begging him to wake up, sobbing and praying, "Jesus, Creator and Spirit, please don't take my brother, I need him more than you do. Please bring him back to me…" he begged, "Please, please…" His mother came and gently peeled him off his brother, and life became a blur for the next few years. Sports relieved some of his emotional pain, but every time he saw a big 18-wheel truck pass by, he thought he just wanted to get on the road and travel, to somehow run from his emotional pain. He realizes he has been doing that same thing most of his life.

* *

Joseph mindlessly enters the grocery store, passing the fresh fruit, looking over at the bananas thinking he had a few muscle cramps recently and was likely low in potassium. He throws a few in the basket. He feels his stomach growl and realizes he is shopping while hungry… He had made a note to himself not to impulse purchase as he finds himself in the deli/bakery looking longingly at the chocolate cheesecake. He wasn't much for sweets, but does love a good cheesecake. He decides to break the impulse hunger urge by calling Jeff and asking him what else he may need for the meal.

"Hey Joseph, hurry home, I am about to light the grill," says Jeff.

"Just thought I would check to see how many are coming to dinner? Did you get us some hot chicks? … Ha" chuckles Joseph.

"Sorry buddy, but a couple of business men I thought you may like to meet are coming. Jacob and his partner, from Cleveland, are looking for a business consultation regarding building a trucking business. Jacob had been on a truck run in North Folk and had some severe pain in his abdomen, and I was on his providers list, so he came in to see me.

When he told me what he does for a living and talked about his dream, I told him to let me know when he would be on his next run and I would invite them over to talk with you. I know you say you are too busy to consider a partner, but that is when people actually need partners, when their business gets so busy," says Jeff a little sheepishly. Joseph doesn't know whether to be offended at his friend's assumption, or relieved about an opportunity. He has been in such a melancholy mood all day, his first instinct is to be angry and hurt, but as he catches himself squeezing a French bread loaf flat, he sees the metaphor of squishing something wonderful. This may be a great opportunity. He quickly throws the bread into the basket, thinking he can use it for Panini sandwiches, and he grabs another for tonight.

He slowly responds to Jeff, "I guess that means enough steak for 4 men?"

"Well, actually, Jacob is big enough for two men, so you better make it enough for five men," he jokes. The tension is gone and Joseph sets his eyes on course looking for the meat section, and picking out the five best T-bones, he talks himself into grabbing a couple of six packs, and then heads to the express checkout line.

He gets close to the driveway of their ranch style suburban house. He notices the yard is sprouting green, but mostly the rearing heads of a variety of weeds rather than grass. He makes a mental note to call the yard care service, to scalp, spray weed prevention, and schedule fertilizing. Spring has sprung right beneath his nose, and he promised Jeff he would make sure the yard is well maintained... *Falling short on several fronts*, he scolded himself. Pulling up in his red Chevy truck, he knows Jeff will be out any moment to help with the groceries. He fooled him today. He actually managed his impulsive purchase habit.

Jeff comes out, "How many bags did you get and how many trips do I need to make?" Joseph has the two bags of groceries and merely instructs Jeff to grab the beer. Jeff whistles, "Wow that is amazing. I sent you to the store and you didn't come home with an entire shopping cart."

"I can control myself, despite what you think," states Joseph with a slight tinge of pride. He has been filling some of his emotional void with impulse purchases recently and Jeff has been concerned.

As they walk in, the good smells of hickory coming in through the open bay door hit Joseph's nostrils and he says, "Can't wait to add the steak to the hickory smell. My mouth is watering already."

"Go get washed up and set the table. Put some beer mugs in the freezer to chill and I will get the steaks on. They just called and are about 10-15 minutes away. I would like to have everything ready and be pulling the steaks off the grill when they get here."

True to Jeff's impeccable timing, he is putting the last steak on the platter when the doorbell rings. Joseph answers the door and isn't expecting to see a big black male starring down at him as he opened the door. He remembered Jeff's comment, but still had not imagined Jacob would be such a "presence." He looks up at Jacob, and as if they were eye to eye, Jacob stuck out his hand, and in a deep, but kind voice introduces himself, "Hello, I am Jacob Jefferson." He quickly steps to the side, and in walks Larry Burger, a skinny redheaded man of a rather short stature. Perhaps he is average in height, but next to Jacob, looks small. Larry smiles a large Dennis the Menace smile, and Joseph immediately feels a genuine liking for both of these men. In the recesses of his mind, he thinks about the odd pair, Laurel and Hardy, and somehow knows these two are oppositely complimentary. Effortlessly he moves aside and both pass by him, led by their noses, with a primitive instinct of men on the trail of a scent.

The wonderful smells of charcoaled steak lead them straight into the enclosed patio dining area. Jeff already has plates, eating ware, napkins, frosted mugs, and brews by each place setting. Enters Jeff, wiping his hands on his apron, and as if on a TV commercial, raises his hands, and says, "Welcome gentleman, enter, Bon Appétite!" With uncanny instinct, the men silently and eagerly sit down, and no words needed... plates filled.

CHAPTER 20

Reflections

Peter Jenkins, despite being tattered from the last few years of PI work, has felt proud managing his life after his wife, Helen left him. He tries to give himself a pep talk, glancing in the window of his car, realizing his hair is matted-up on top of his head…and he just looks wrinkled. Despite his laughter at Peter Faulk on Colombo, overall he admired his tactical skills. In fact, he is likely one of his inspirations prompting him into investigative work. He certainly didn't plan on growing up and being almost a clone replica! He grumbles to himself that Helen just didn't know what she was missing. He is in complete denial about his unsavory lifestyle and disposition. She worked at a local coffee shop and went to nursing school to better her life. He recalls her pretty, ivory skin, and hazel green eyes, that looked at him with such high regard. He recounts how she had told him she thought perhaps the night and weekend work would match Peter's PI work. He knew he stayed out late or sometimes all night, and often would sleep in the car while staking out a place to catch some photos. He hoped his work would progress from the fieldwork, which included primarily blue-collar workers attempting to catch a wife or husband having an affair so they may have the upper hand in the divorce process.

* *

Peter grabs a coffee and donut at Dunk the Donut, and tries to console himself. He pushes the thought of gambling away most of his wife, or ex-wife's, savings account. That was her final straw. Well, she may regret leaving him. This latest job might just put him in the big league. She might run back to him, if he ends up working for some bigwig politicians. Peter, the PI, heads over to Parties and Weddings by DeBoe. After he botched up tailing Jorge, he asks Mr. Fisher if he can keep an eye on DeBoe's place, to see if Maria shows up there. John, although angry, calling Peter a few choice words, is desperate to find Maria, so he agrees to give Peter another chance.

Jorge denies seeing Maria, and in fact, acts worried he has not heard from her. John knows, instinctively Maria would not have gone for 3 days without talking to Jorge, but John feels trapped between a rock and a hard place. His historical strategies of threatening Jorge have been dissipating over the last couple of years and John is beginning to feel like a fish in a fishbowl ever since he began running for the Senate. He has had several news reporters show up at a variety of locations and, like roaches, can be annoying and creep around, when you least expect it. He has to put on his happy family man mask, and finds himself commenting that his wife is away in Mexico, taking care of a sickly aunt. He has been concerned about his wife's Hispanic background, and being first generation as a U.S. citizen. On the contrary, with the controversy of immigration, the Republican Party wants to run on the coattail of that theme. They feel having a candidate who is more empathetic with immigration will offer their party one more seat in the U.S. Senate. This will not be a time for Maria to leave him. He will do whatever he needs to do to make sure she stays.

Peter starts watching the shop for any unusual activity. He notices a pretty, blonde-haired person leaving the building with several crates she pulls out on a dolly. It is before hours, and he finds that that seems strange. The morning spring air is still a bit nippy, and he sips his coffee, but does not notice that he did not put the plastic lid on right. The steamy, sugary substance falls straight into his crotch. Startled, he lets out a howl, and jerks his hand in time for most of it to splash all over him. He is burned and sticky. In his pain and exasperation, he reaches into the back seat to grab one of his old and dusty handy dandy towels. It may have been white some time back, but now, covered in dusty muck.

Wiping himself off, he fails to notice the small burgundy minivan leaving the curb and heading through the ally way. He is laughably nasty in appearance, with his white shirt bathed in brown and his crotch wet. He puts what is left of his coffee on the seat, with the rest rolling down onto all of his paperwork he so diligently put together last night. It is all of his notes he had taken related to the potential whereabouts of of Maria. The only thing on his mind is finding that minivan. As Sarah, obliviously listens to early morning music and weather details for the day, little did she know, Mr. Peter, the PI, has lost her trail. She says her usual Hail Mary, but adds a special prayer for Maria, knowing she is feeling the pressure from being "missing."

John is becoming more impatient by the minute... his nights, filled with restless fits, and painful memories. He phones Peter early to note any progress made regarding Maria's whereabouts. The PI sees Mr. Fisher's number on the caller ID and realizes it would be better to let it go to voice mail than tell him he has lost the trail of the minivan. He couldn't help that he spilled hot coffee down his pants.

He has researched Sarah, Ms. DeBoe's most recent designer employee. Her background is void of any dirt; in fact, she seems like a pretty, wholesome dame. Most of her Face Book posts are about design, art, and religion. Based on what is said about Maria, they will be a good team. He isn't convinced threats to disclose some devious history will make her cooperate with his investigation. He thinks he will likely get results if he tells her the family is worried about her whereabouts, and the story of being in Mexico is merely a cover-up. Then he will add to his ploy... if she could offer any information, the family will be eternally grateful. Yes, he is confident this will work! *She is one of those saintly do-gooders!* It never dawns on Peter that perhaps Maria does not want anyone to find her...and with good reason!

Since Peter has nothing else to do with his day, he decides he better not fumble this case. He, instead, sits there all day, in his crumbled clothing stained with coffee. He sits there, lies there, and moves in any other position he can dream up. He has been a PI for years and done many overnight watches, but he is not getting any younger and his bones and joints keep talking to him and reminding him of his age.

Meanwhile, Sarah arrives at the warehouse, greeted by Maria, who looks distressed. Sarah, being very intuitive, grabs Maria by the arm, leads her into the warehouse office and lowers her into a chair.

"What has happened, you look like you have seen a ghost?" Maria proceeds to speak half in Spanish and English with a little Spanglish, until Sarah is very confused.

"Slow down Maria… what has happened?" Maria takes a deep breath, attempting to compose herself, but then begins to pace and wave her arms around hysterically.

She said, "I spoke with Jorge who said, "Mom, Dad is looking like a crazed maniac… I think he is the craziest I have ever seen him. He swears if he finds you and you don't come back to him, then no one will ever see you again." Maria said, "Jorge told me he tried to record John, and John grabbed his phone. Now, if John gets past the lock on the phone, he will realize I am still in the city."

John takes the phone to his office and is about to request one of the IT guys from the firm to check on how to break in past the password, when Peter the PI calls. Peter rambles to John about how he has been tracking the van all day but just now is having an opportunity to go and interview Ms. Sarah. He lies about his day, but he feels confident it will be a good opportunity for the do-gooder to give him some information to keep him on Maria's trail. John is not buying his story but Peter PI is the closest thing to finding out some information he needs to track Maria's whereabouts. Meanwhile…

Sarah calmly tells Maria to give her Jorge's phone number and Maria begins to talk in Spanish, but catches herself, and slows down to English. "I am not sure what phone he called me from pero John may have mi numero de telephone." Sarah takes Maria's phone and has her open the phone log. She readily dials the last number on the log.

She hears on the other end, "Hello, Jorge's Whore House, how may I help you?" Sarah clears her throat. Jorge says, "Mom, I just thought I would lighten your mood and help you worry about me instead of Dad."

Sarah says with a pleasantly offended voice, "This is Sarah; I work with your mother. She is very upset and fearful that John may get information from the phone that could lead him here. Did you shut that phone off?" Jorge feels stupid. What is wrong with him not to think of that? He says, "I was just about to do that... How is mom by the way?" Sarah can feel the concern in his voice so she pardons his warped humor and hands the phone to Maria.

Jorge reassures her he will shut that phone off and he will call her later on a new phone. Right now, he is borrowing a friend's phone for the day. He hangs up and immediately calls the phone company.

Peter the PI is nodding in and out of consciousness, and cursing when he wakes up and his knees or arms are hitting the steering wheel, he is barely cognizant, but does hear the rumble of a van. He smacks himself in the face to clear his hazy visibility. He has forgotten his glasses once again. Yes, there the van is again, and out walks Ms. Sarah Sabeans. He doesn't waste any time, but jumps out of his car and rushes towards her.

Sarah, trained in some martial arts is about to respond in an automatic response which would likely have landed Peter PI on the ground. Fortunately for him, he has enough training to recognize a defensive posture and whips out his handy dandy detective ID. Feeling like Devil Dog finding a villainous criminal, he says with authority, "Ma'am, I am Peter Jenkins, a Private Investigator, needing to ask you a few questions related to the missing person, Maria Fisher."

Sarah can hardly keep a straight face. She wonders whether this is some kind of a joke, but doesn't want to offend this guy. Could he be for real? She decides she will placate his urgent and disheveled appearance. Feeling confident that she can take him out in about two seconds if needed, she asks him to come into the shop. She makes sure to steer him through the hallway that has evening security guards just coming on night rounds. Besides, it is away from any of the valuable materials or clothing he may soil with just a brush of his filthy clothing. She has a notion to stop by an area that has some sample cologne to freshen him up a little. She feels lightheaded just thinking about being in a closed area with him. However, it will be better to get him out ASAP. She does not want to accidentally slip and give him any information.

She remembers taking a couple of classes in criminology for the heck of it, since most of her major courses were her delight; she figured some variety would ultimately benefit her. There was something said in one of her classes about answering questions with questions as the best offensive defense. She would try it.

Mr. Jenkins sits across the room from Sarah and pulls out a pocket notepad, and pen. He begins, "Do you know Maria Fisher."

She responds, "How do you mean, know her?"

Taken back, "Well, I mean do you work with her."

Sarah says, "Is there some problem?"

He answers her question, "Well, she is missing."

Sarah continues, "Do you know where she is?"

He is feeling a bit confused, "I was going to ask you the same thing?"

She is getting into this play write, "You mean she is missing and you don't know where she is? What sort of detective are you? Coming to the place where she works and not having any news of her whereabouts, what were you thinking?" He is unsure why, but he is feeling very defensive and flustered. Perhaps it is because he woke from a deep sleep? He is not getting anywhere, fast.

He tries to gain her sympathy, "Mr. Fisher is very worried about her and is trying to find out some information on her whereabouts."

Sarah immediately interjects question after question, never answering a single question… "Did you check with her son? Did you contact her family in Mexico? How is her son doing? Have you spoken with Ms. DeBoe? …" …And on and on. Peter's head is spinning. He can only think about getting away from this barrage of questions. He abruptly dismisses himself and heads back to his car, bewildered at what just happened. Sarah is relieved, but feels bemused that her criminal justice class actually held some merit. Feeling a little arrogant, she lifts up her cross and says a brief prayer of gratitude she did not have to lie.

CHAPTER 21

Sue is on her second day with the girls. The first evening went well, after bombarding her with a multitude of questions and perpetual chatter. Sue is able to find her way into her mother's bedroom and change the sheets, as she stumbles over clothes and shoes. It takes her back to the years of living at home, perpetually cleaning up after everyone. She is able to hold off the girls from changing clothes in the same room as well as them not hearing her having bouts of nausea. She keeps the radio on in her mother's room as well as the fan running in the bathroom. She wakes up in the morning with quiet whispers in the living room. Her sisters are anything but quiet when they are with her and she does not remember them having much consideration for others sleeping. She stretches a bit, puts on her floppy robe and attempts to nonchalantly, investigate why they are whispering. Sue tip toes down the hall as she hears the muffled voices, and peeks around the corner, but right as she is about to get a full view of her sisters, Ginger whines and wags her tail and both girls get up abruptly and block her view of what they were doing on the sofa. They both grab her arms and usher her around the side hall to the kitchen.

Their voices now raised to usual high frequencies are begging Sue to cook them some of her delicious omelets. She puts the concern in a file, "to be investigated later," and allows herself to just enjoy being with her sisters. She puts on a tea instead of the coffee pot and the girls give one another a knowing look.

Sylvia chimes up, "What, we aren't getting coffee? Since when are we living like the English?" Sue has become accustomed to having herbal tea over the last several weeks since coffee would make her sick and give her indigestion. She forgets her sisters love her coffee. Sylvia goes to the cabinet, pulls out the step stool, finds the coffee grinder in the back of the cabinet and grabs a new bag of specialty coffee beans from the pantry. "I bought this good coffee from a specialty shop because I knew you were going to fix us some good coffee. You know Mom sticks to Folgers and says that is coffee she used when a waitress in high school."

The challenge catches Sue off guard and she stumbles for a rebuttal. "Well, I decided coffee is making me too anxious and since I would have enough stress being here with you two, I should bring some herbal tea."

Sarah looks at her with hurt, and says, "You sound just like Mom, always blaming us for any changes or things she doesn't like."

Sue does not recognize, that despite her efforts to avoid acting like her mother, she sounds just like her. Just like Sam, when she feels pressure or defensive, she finds another to blame. She reddens in the face, both from humiliation at being caught acting like her mother, and from not telling the truth. "I am so sorry girls; I should not have said that. I hate sounding like mother."

Sylvia appears reflective, and says, "I know, it is hard not to be like our mother in some way or another. I seem to always need male attention and sometimes I feel guilty for the clothes I wear, but the boys notice me and flirt with me when I look like that." Sue realizes she has been away from the girls most of the last year or so and has failed to recognize this going on in front of her eyes. Guilt floods over her like an unexpected storm beating the new spring flowers down. She knows immediately her sister is telling her indirectly she is sleeping around. Seconds feel like hours, wrestling inside if the topic needs to discuss later. After all, who is she to speak of responsible sexuality? She is pregnant out of wedlock and not involved with the father at all.

Before the microseconds formed into a tangible action, Sylvia leans over the counter and says, "Do you have something to tell us Sis?"

Sue turns around to get some eggs and milk out of the fridge, while she simultaneously attempts to grind coffee for the girls. She responds with, "I don't think so, why?"

Sarah states, "We found a book about pregnancy in your overnight bag on the couch."

Sylvia throws a nearby sofa pillow at Sarah. "Shut up, I wanted her to tell us on her own!"

Sue composed, with a rehearsed conviction, "No, the book is for Latisha, I heard she is pregnant and wanted to bring her this book when I came here."

Sylvia gazes at Sue with catlike eyes, looking straight into her soul. "Really, I thought you told me she has a bakery in Cleveland? Why would you bring that all the way here?" Fortunately, Sue spoke with Latisha right before she came and found out that news, as well as she was going to be attending a cake-baking workshop in Maryland this week.

Latisha is at a workshop here, in the city and I wanted to surprise her with it when we go out to lunch. The girls do not look completely convinced, but for the moment are placated. Sue realizes this may be more difficult to keep secret than she had thought. It is the beginning of big events for the girls so Sue, while finishing the breakfast, asks Sarah if she has her parts rehearsed and is confident about her role in the play. Then not to miss a beat and give equal attention to both girls, she adds, "Speaking of ready, do you have all you need for graduation tomorrow night, Sylvia?"

Both girls start talking simultaneously, each one interrupting the other. Then they break out in laughter, and Sue feels the tension release from the air knowing she has slipped by for now. She also realizes her sisters will be very hurt when they find out she lied to them. For now, she is unable to convince herself it is the right thing to do. Her instinct tries to remind her that lies will catch up with her, and it is better to have her sisters as allies. She simply does not have the heart to have them feel her burden or worry about her when they have so many positive things going on for them. She rationalizes it is best for them.

She does a little running around with the girls, listens to Sarah's perfectly rehearsed script, and then has the afternoon to herself, from 1-6pm. She pulls out her phone and calls Latisha to see if she wants to meet for a while, so she will only be telling a half lie. Latisha surprisingly answers the phone. "Hey Latisha, this is Sue and guess what? I am in Maryland, and was hoping you may have some time to hang out and grab a bite to eat."

"Really… Oh, my goodness… my workshop ended at 1pm and does not start again until the evening session from 6-9pm. All of the instructors have to prep for their evening shifts and do not return until 5:30pm. I was feeling big, fat, and trapped in my hotel room." Sue felt it must be providence, and as Latisha gives her directions, she realizes her hotel is just 5 minutes from Jerry's Pizza and Sub shop.

She pulls out his business card to double check, and sure enough, there it is right off the same interstate. She gets a surge of collective energy in her stomach, unlike the morning sickness, or little one swirling around; it is a sensation of excitement she felt when they got tangled up in Ginger's rope just a few days earlier. Was that only a few days ago? She tells Latisha she will pick her up in 45 minutes and jumps up to get ready. She does not usually primp, and figures he is the one person that knows she is pregnant, so she will risk going a la natural. She throws on some clothes and heads out the door. She looks briefly in the mirror, and pulls out some lipstick from her purse. Her cheeks are naturally rosy these days. She has on loose jeans and a sweatshirt. Her hair is thick and down. She talks to herself, *You are still young and allowed to have fun and adventure…"*

Sue hears Ginger whine and realizes she needs to put her in the back yard. Darn, she is pushing 45 min. She will have to speed a little to get there. Ginger, extra happy with the girls giving her attention, easily goes outside, where they have already made her a comfortable makeshift bed from an old comforter. She has several chew toys and bones. It is amazing how much they have spoiled her in two days.

She plugs the address into her Google maps and buckles in. She is several miles down the road and has a chance to ponder her thoughts. It has been several days since she has thought much about Jorge. She wonders if he has given her any thought, and as if by telepathy, her phone begins to chime. She has on her Bluetooth, so she can keep her hands on the wheel of her car. For whatever reason, she doesn't look at the phone and she just answers it.

A pleasant and sexy voice says, "Hello Sue, this is Jorge, please don't hang up on me. I have been calling and calling and I have been worried about you."

A strange sensation of aloof confidence comes over her as if her subconscious is telling her she has done this on her own this far and she certainly does not need him now. "Oh, Jorge, how are you? I have been really busy and am about to go meet up with my friend Latisha."

"So, I am confused, I heard you are visiting your sisters, but you are here in Cleveland?" he questions.

"So, you really are checking up on me…" she smugly replies. "Who gave you that information?" Sue already knows the answer. It had to be Diane since she has been communicating with Jorge.

"I spoke with Diane several times after our misunderstanding. I have wanted desperately to hear your voice and see you. I really miss you."

Sue, not buying Jorge's bullshit, says, "Oh really, I believe last time we had a potentially civil conversation, you told me I was annoying you."

He briefly recalls the day she was speaking of and remembers feeling agitated and annoyed that day. Rather than making excuses, or blame shifting, he remembers the words of his mother 'Treat them like a cherished rose'. "I am so sorry; I was uptight about preparing for my law school interview. I can be a jerk sometimes."

Sue remembers her sister's comments about her being like her mother. She expects them to forgive her. She does not have to be perpetually hurt and defensive. "O.K. I forgive you, but I have since moved on Jorge. It has been quite a while since I went out with you. Things change."

"Does that mean you are with someone else?" She isn't really, but has some immediate guilt she is about to go and see Jerry. Why can't she just be like Diane and just move on or even see a couple of guys at the same time? The thought of Diane makes her feel angry. She retorts, "I am not like Diane, jumping from one guy to the next!"

'Hmm,' thought Jorge *this might be the time for a little mutual indignation.* "I know what you mean about Diane, I went to her house to inquire about your whereabouts, and I thought she was going to eat me alive." Jorge says, while remembering Diane's catlike qualities.

"Really, so how many other times have you SEEN my so called Best Friend?" Sue snarls with unexpected jealous venom.

"Wow, don't worry, I told her I knew you and she are best friends and I assured her I did not want anything to come between you two," he appeals to her need to belong… "After all, I know you struggled to be on your own for a long time and certainly don't have much of a mother to lean on." She has the old familiar feeling of hurt, defensiveness, and need heard hit her, and her chest and neck begin to tighten.

She breaths and calms herself, trying to finish the conversation before she has a panic attack. "Look Jorge, I liked our time together, but it has been too long, and I don't know if I can see you again. I have a lot going on. Today I am going to visit with Latisha, and then see a new friend I recently met."

Jorge catches the moment, "Diane told me Latisha is pregnant, does the father of the baby know she is pregnant? That is tough. I hope she tells the father. Every guy should have a chance to know if he is going to be a father!"

Sue is speechless… Here she is carrying his child and he doesn't know a thing about it. She decides to use this as a time to pry a little bit. "What makes you think a woman should tell the man, especially if they are not together? Besides, women have to weigh their options without the pressure of an uninvolved man," Sue says.

Jorge is enjoying the dialogue and senses he really has missed Sue's independent and opinionated disposition. He continues, "So, are you saying Latisha is considering an abortion? That is not as common in the black community; although she does have a white mother." Sue finds herself agitated he is sounding like an indifferent attorney, with some racial biases. She realizes she has heard enough and just wants to get off the phone.

"Jorge, look, it is over between us. Congratulations, you already sound like a cold-hearted bigoted attorney. Now I have to go, I am trying to keep my mind on driving. I hope you have a good life and good luck with your precious law career," she says, with a little sting. She knew that was a little dig because he had told her several times he was unsure about law as a career, but felt it was what he had to do to please his father. She is further aware, because he played football; many of his close friends are African American. She hangs up, a little flustered and confused. Jorge, feeling a little sting from her unwarranted comments, is certain he opened some sort of heart area, because Sue has never deliberately vicious. In the law field, if people become defensive, it usually means you have hit a soft spot and they are vulnerable. That last comment meant he is getting to her. He will give her a few days and then re-approach. He needs another strategy, but is unsure what.

The entire conversation has created stress and confusion in Sue. The waves seem to fill her womb with some sort of toxicity. The feeling of detachment begins. A sense of feeling unwanted, the bright twinkle begins going dim; but as quickly as the spark diminishes, it glows again. Sue realizes whether Jorge ever knows or is ever involved with this child, she will be born and loved. *Little One* twirls in the womb, feels a light sense of purpose... perhaps a message from Source... She exists; she is here for a reason.

Sue finally navigates to the restaurant to meet Latisha, who is currently sitting by herself near a large window overlooking a golf course. She is looking out the window as if lost in a sea of thought. Sue stands there watching her friend, knowing exactly what she is feeling.

She wonders how far along Latisha is right now and how she is handling the rumor mill. Sue deliberately makes a loud exclamation at seeing her friend, Latisha. Sue does not feel embarrassed, but observes from afar. Latisha looks up startled, as if coming out of a trance. Latisha gets up out of the booth and embraces her childhood friend. She immediately begins to sob, and Sue gently guides her into the booth and sits right beside her as if long lost lovers.

Latisha says, shyly, "Well, I guess you have heard the news, along with everyone else I know. Man, news travels fast and everyone has opinions." "Latisha, you should abort that baby. You know you cannot run your shop while raising a child. Latisha, you should put the baby up for adoption. There are many people, wanting children who cannot have them... "Latisha this and Latisha that" ... I am tired of peoples' opinions. Opinions are like belly buttons, everyone has one." She can still be quite funny, despite her drama.

She continues to talk aloud, as if to the world at large. "I am just saying, I am glad for my parents. They are letting me take my time to decide what to do, and have said, "Whatever you decide, we will help to support you." My Dad may be big, but he loves me, and I need that right now!" Sue has a wave of sadness hit her in the gut, as well as little one feeling the pain, her stomach jolts with a sense of aloneness. Sue's expression must be loud because Latisha says, "I am sorry, I know your Dad is not around. At least you don't have to go through this type of ordeal like facing your father, and being without the father of the baby. That would be more than a girl could bear!" The tables turn, and Sue bursts out into tears, and Latisha is uncertain where she went wrong in this conversation and who should be comforting whom?

"Sue, what is wrong with you? What did I say, Geez, I am sorry! I am the one who should be crying, not you..."

Sue bursts out, without any forethought, "I am pregnant, too!"

O.K. now Latisha is confused. "What? Why haven't you called me girl? I thought you haven't talked to me because you were mad I got pregnant, and didn't want to lecture me. "When, who, and what" Instead of crying, Latisha bursts out laughing, and then, as if it is contagious, Sue shifts from tears to hysterical laughter. The waiter is standing there with his pad and paper, not knowing if he should continue to stand there, or if he should exit, back to the kitchen and resurface in a few minutes.

They are embracing one another, when Sue catches a glimpse from the corner of her eye of the waiter about to walk away. She says, "If you will leave the menus with us for a few minutes, I promise we will compose ourselves and you can get our orders."

He smiles with some relief having a clear direction to proceed... No one ever taught him how to manage these sorts of female hormones. Crying one minute and laughing the next. He vaguely remembers his father telling him, "Son, you never know which way a women's mood may turn. They can be like a cloud, soft and fluffy one minute and stormy with lightning bolts the next." Wow, was that ever true with these two. He walks away shaking his head, and the two young women continue with their embrace until the emotions settle. There is much to discuss.

The girls are back into feeling like little children exploring together. They both have had so many similar ideas, thoughts, sensations, and most of all, feelings of aloneness in the process. It is an exhilarating perspective, to have one of your best friends experiencing pregnancy. The relief is unbelievable. As much as the sense of aloneness was overpowering, the sense of belonging is suddenly very empowering. They mindlessly order their meal; discuss options, thoughts, the lack of involvement of the sperm donors, etc.

Before they know it, the hour has flown by and they must depart. Both assure one another of the secrecy of Sue's pregnancy. Sue does say she will allow Latisha to tell her father. She has such fond memories of Jacob's paternal role in her life. At least she may sense there is some fatherly blessing coming her way. Somehow, she knows he will understand.

Sue springs to her car. Well as much as a pregnant girl can bounce. She feels such relief and now has someone she can call anytime. In fact, she feels needed by her friend as much as she needs her. Who would have ever thought after the conflicted emotions with Jorge, she would sense such a lift of spirit. Today is just full of surprises. She has one more surprise. She did not tell Jerry she is stopping by. She decided to leave that to fate. If he is around, it is supposed to be… and if not, oh well. She is tired of trying to control everything. It is obvious she has very little control of much of anything!

She is reasonably close to Jerry's Pizza shop and knows it is mid-afternoon, when he is not too busy. Sue parks her car on the side of the shop, and before she can talk herself out of stopping by, she unbuckles her seat belt, freshens up her lipstick, lets her hair loose out of the ponytail, and runs her hand through it. She feels a brief knot in her gut, but attributes that to the Chicken Alfredo she just ate. She is tired of thinking so much. For once, she needs to be impromptu.

Sue walks into the shop, wearing a loose fitting tee shirt and jeans that are snug these days. Fortunately, Latisha has grown out of some of her maternity clothes, and said she will gladly pass them on. Despite feeling a bit frumpy, she has been eating conscientiously and now her "glow" is even visible to herself. He is at the register, looking over the counter, talking to a customer, so Sue stops and looks at some of the historical photos on the wall. She had not noticed these before. Jerry has black and white photos of his grandmother in front of a big pizza oven, pulling out a pizza. There is another one of her taking a bite of a pizza. There are a few articles about his grandmother's shop, secret pizza dough recipe, and finally a few write-ups from local newspapers celebrating his grand opening.

She has her back turned to Jerry, and he comes up behind her and taps her on the shoulder, saying, "Can I help you Miss?" As soon as she turns around, he steps back, takes a deep gasp and then without a second thought, he scoops her up in a big embrace. Before she has a thought in her mind, she mutually embraces him and as their faces meet, both realize what they have just done, and loosen the embrace, but it is a slow release for both of them. The few seconds feel like hours as their eyes meet and recognition of their previous soul connection bleeds through their emotional sensations.

Sue smiles her coquettish smile, and Jerry whistles, and pulls her back from himself, holding her hands the entire time. "Wow, I can see the pregnancy glow, you look absolutely beautiful." She doesn't object, but finds herself lapping up the flow of his compliments like an unquenchable thirst for acknowledgement of her pregnancy. Latisha opened Pandora's Box. She has an urge to talk about the pregnancy, and her experiences. She had not realized until a little over an hour ago, how much she has stuffed inside. She is overflowing with information, and like many females, but untypical of herself, she begins rambling nonstop, "I just met with a friend of mine, and she is pregnant and non-committed. We were able to talk about the feelings of shame, uncertainty, what we are going to do, and just everything I can think of."

Jerry is amused and taken back at the same time. No one is in the shop right now, but he really feels this conversation deserves some privacy as well as his full attention. He gently leads Sue to a table and says, "Let me get you a drink and see if Tommy is available to watch the shop while we go over to the house so I can listen to you." Sue senses her old feelings of caution, even paranoia creeping in; as she feels the reality, setting in that Jerry wants to take her next door to his home. She is not expecting this response, but then again, she did not expect herself to gush out emotional slosh to someone she barely knows. She freezes up and is the clammy Sue Jerry first met. He immediately realizes the offer may seem excessively entitled on his part. He states, "O.K. I can see that offer was over the top for you. What would be a better option for you? I just want to propose some privacy, which is not guaranteed in here."

Sue feels the tension release in her neck and shoulders, and realizes she has almost been holding her breath. She remembers to breath diaphragmatically to calm down the panic sensation. She read that in one of her self-help books about managing anxiety responses. It is more difficult to breathe this way as her diaphragm is beginning to feel pressure from the ever-growing uterus. However, after a few deep breaths, with exhaling more than inhaling, she feels almost normal again. He patiently waits for her response. He has an uncanny way about knowing what she wants and needs. She feels tended to, for once in her life. She clears her throat, and says, "I would feel comfortable to go out by that beautiful tree where we managed to get entangled in Ginger's strap."

He smiles, remembering the enchanting moments that he has not been able to get out of his mind. "O.K. Let me grab a blanket and we can go sit out there. It is just the right temperature for being outside anyway." He shuffles around the corner and is back before she can think to resist the idea again.

He leads her by the hand and she feels surreal. The sun is just right, the wind is mildly breezy and his hand is warm and enticing. Jerry places the large plaid quilted blanket on the ground, making sure it is on a grassy spot rather than over the dirt and roots around the tree. He mumbles the blanket was hand quilted by his grandmother and he doesn't want it to get too dirty. He considerately brought a pillow and fluffed it up, leaning it against the tree for Sue. He is a gentle man and tenderly helps her get comfortable.

She gets the keen sense he has been around this before and asks him, "Where did you learn to be so intuitive about pregnant women?"

Jerry takes a few deep breaths and sighs, "Well, I am the oldest of three, and the younger two are my little sisters. They both left home when they were young to get away from my controlling father. Since I do not have any children of my own, when my sisters became pregnant, I made it my job to assist them in any way possible. The youngest one has a two-year-old, so it hasn't been too long. Jessica is 24 years old. I would guess she was about your age when she delivered Thomas. The older one, Marianna, is 26 years old, two years younger than me.

Therefore, that makes me the old man of the family. I feel somewhat responsible for them and always watched out after them when we were kids. It has been particularly hard on Marianna since her husband is in the National Guard and recently deployed to Afghanistan. He doesn't go often, but when he does, it is really hard on her to manage Jeremiah, and Joshua."

Sue is enjoying the dialogue. Until today, she had almost forgotten what just chatting with a friend feels like. He is confiding in her and does not seem to have any agenda. She mentally notes this. The last couple of weeks she was with Jorge, it seemed he was constantly talking about his accomplishments, pursuits and on occasion, frustrations with repetitively disappointing his father. He is an only child, so it is nice to talk to an older sibling. She definitely can relate to his feelings of being responsible for his younger sisters. Isn't that what she feels about her sisters? Diane, well that is an entire other can of worms. Has she really even been a friend? She chooses to put her out of her mind, like an unreachable itch, you have to ignore it and it will go away. Perhaps the feelings of betrayal will go away if she just ignores it.

At least an hour goes by and she realizes she is supposed to be home for her sister's activities. It is already getting around 4pm, so she has an hour and a half to get home and get dressed, ready for the evening. He helps her up and she stretches and then has to pick up the pace. She is forward focused and hopes her abrupt departure won't dampen the wonderful visit they just had. She only has a few more days in the area and is sure she won't see Jerry again anyway. She gives her salutations and explains as she gets into the car, putting on her seatbelt, that the girls are having activities and she has to make it back in time.

Jerry feels some tugging on his heartstrings, but understands having to be the surrogate parent figure. He was that for much of his adult life. His father was a grouchy workaholic, never attending anything of any of the kids. His mother is a reclusive, Xanax addict, who functions on only a few sober brain cells in a day. Her consistent anxiety and agoraphobia, lead to years of addiction to prescription medication.

He can definitely excuse her abrupt departure. If it were him, he would have done the same thing. He waves and realizes he never obtained any contact information, and doesn't even know her last name. He feels a bit helpless, but lets it go as he sees his parking lot is filling up and is certain Tommy is in need of his services. He rushes in, puts on his apron, and gets to work, putting Sue into the back of his mind, to think about later.

CHAPTER 22

Joseph feels a little nervous, but excited at the same time. He has dreamed of having a partner, but to think, he is looking at two partners. Each brings to the table their own set of talents, and skills. Jacob has a background in business management, but after his white-collar crime, he has been unable to get back into the corporate world. It resulted in truck driving. When he met Larry, the relationship was cordial, but Larry's persistence led Jacob to sharing some of his history and dreams. Jacob had been looking into the latest security computer trackers utilized in Limo companies as well as other major transit companies. It is on the cusp of having the major thrust move from the GS2 to the GS3. He believes if he can get this product to trucking companies, that it can save thousands of dollars a year. He needs funding and Larry is the man with the money and technical background. Their vision has grown and now they want to be a direct part of a trucking company. This is when Sparks and Associates, LLC is brought to their attention by Dr. Jeff.

Reflections

He has an odd series of events that have left him feeling a little unnerved. He had another dream with the Indian woman. On that night, he recalls being in a dark swampland and the woman comes out from behind a tree and takes him by the hand leading him in the dark, as he cannot see anything, he feels comfortable as long as she is holding his hand. She lets go of his hand, and he feels a sense of helplessness as he desperately looks around. Up and out of nowhere, he simultaneously sees and hears a rattlesnake coming straight at him to strike him. He feels helpless when the Indian woman appears, and tosses him an old-fashioned razor. He cuts the head off the snake as it is about to strike him. He finds himself in the daylight, in his car, looking in the rearview mirror and he wakes up startled.

As he is now aware of dream meanings, he has been less frightened and somewhat intrigued. He looks up rattlesnake and it can represent the passage of time, a razor can mean a problem needs "to be smoothed out," rearview mirror can mean hurts from the past, and daylight can mean clarity. He can see the message he is getting about his past, and clearing it up. He wonders if these two new partners may help him to move forward and let go of some of his unresolved issues. It seems Jacob has moved past his hurts; he could certainly learn a few things from him.

**

He meets with the two of them several more times, including his last visit in Cleveland and to Jacob's home. During the visit, he mentions his daughter and despite her being pregnant out of wedlock, he is looking forward to being a grandfather. He seems jollier than ever. Joseph figures his daughter would be about the same age, and mentions it would be nice to be a grandfather. When Jacob asks him if he has any children, he hesitates, and then denies it. He can see in Jacob's eyes; this will not be the end of this conversation. He feels an urgency to speak further to Jacob, but feelings of shame and fear grip him. He does not want to muddy the water of a blossoming business relationship with personal matters. He keeps his history a secret from everyone but Jeff. Jeff has taken a vow not to let anyone know Joseph's history. His secret is safe, at the same time, he feels his Indian Princess visitations getting more frequent, and is sure they will not relent until he takes some active steps to right his wrongs.

CHAPTER 23

John, pacing around his office, is unsure if it has reached the point of telling Jake, his campaign manager, what has really happened with Maria. Jake enters in and says, "We really are being pressured by the media for an interview with your wife. Part of your platform for this candidacy is advocating for immigration and your wife is a first generation, and can generate some empathy and relatedness for the Latino vote. It is imperative to have her respond. If she is with her sick aunt in Mexico, perhaps we can get her to a café with WIFI and we can do a Skype interview recording? I have a script of the questions as well as suggested answers. Of course... she can put it in her own words, but it will be the basics of what would touch the hearts and bring the votes, if you know what I mean. The basic script says, 'The fear my parents have faced as immigrants has caused undo anxiety. Fortunately, they were able to gain citizenship. However, there are approximately 11 million undocumented immigrants that need this reform to offer them opportunity for citizenship.'"

John cannot bring himself to tell Jake his wife left him and is hiding from him. He cannot bear to inform him his wife had divorce papers served and with it, there was a brief note from Judge Sanchez, who says, "I have observed over the years, the bruises and marks on Maria. She has informed me of what has happened in your family household. She has evidence to support these allegations. I have influence. I suggest you let her follow through with the divorce or I will make this information public. It would not look good for your political campaign."

The phone rings and Peter is on the other end. He has taken the past several days following not only Sarah, but DeBoe. Sarah, ended up at a warehouse and would always park in the front parking area while he noticed when Ms. DeBoe arrived, she parked in an area around back, not visible from the road. He finally concluded there was someone else in the warehouse, when he noticed Sarah coming outside, interacting as the door was closing, despite no other car being in the parking lot. Peter is excited to call Mr. Fisher about his recent find, and feels confident he will find Maria shortly. He calls Mr. Fisher and can sense Mr. Fisher's immediate frustration at his absence. He explains to him his discoveries and senses he is close on the trail of Maria.

John's predatory instincts kick in and he is keenly aware he has to find Maria and convince her to return, even just through the campaign. He cannot bear to live without her, but she also has the power to destroy his future. It has been almost humorous to think, after all of these years; Maria holds the power over him. He quickly informs Peter, the PI; he appreciates his dedication on the case, but will no longer need his services. He will pay him an extra $500, and he can pick up his check and he will write a referral letter if needed. Peter, taken aback by feeling dismissed and discounted, only wants to finish his job and find Maria. Peter lets Mr. Fisher know he does not want the extra money, but to merely feel the satisfaction of completing his work. At this point John Fisher's patience has come to the end of its rope. He growls, "Listen you little shit, I don't need your services anymore, and if you continue with anything, I will ruin your name." He hangs up on Peter.

Peter may be many things, but he is not a quitter, and is determined to find Maria. He believes Mr. Fisher will ultimately appreciate him when he is able to talk Maria into coming to the office and meeting with Mr. Fisher. He fails to see, like his ex-wife; Maria is done with the talking; and just wants to move forward in life. Unlike his ex-wife, Maria suffered not only emotional bruises, but also physical bruises. For Maria, there is no turning back.

Maria hums to herself and puts some final changes on the last project for the Shoreline advertising. A mixture of metal, statues, and florescent lighting, the masterpiece will have a dazzling invitation for the new shopping area. She takes a deep breath and looks around, noticing and appreciating her environment. She has felt a little cooped up but is aware the legal process can be long and arduous. Judge Sanchez has assured her he will contact her as he receives the signature on the divorce papers and John has secured representation. She stops to admire her surroundings, and realizes how blessed she is to have a luxurious loft apartment right here in the warehouse. Plush, with leopard, gold, black and silver touches, making the area seemed elegant. It is something she would create for someone else but not herself.

Reflections

She has had time to process and ponder some of her experiences. Maria is beginning to recognize she feels guilty for most things that go wrong… In fact, John consistently blames her for his mood, and any outcome that turns out badly. He almost convinced her she was responsible for the miscarriage. He said if she would have taken Jorge with her instead of him picking him up from school, he wouldn't have been angry and then she would not have fallen…it is her fault she lost the baby. She remembered she had been on the verge of suicide, when she fell on her knees and began to pray.

She continues to recount how she pulled out the dusty bible from the shelf and found several passages. "All have sinned and come short of the glory of God… His strength is made perfect in your weakness… by grace are you saved through faith, not of your own works." She felt a flood of peace and the exit plan began to formulate. It has taken four years to get the plan in place, and here she is, afraid, but excited at having a future free of terror, blame, and pain. Well, she may suffer, most likely will suffer, but at least it won't be by John's hands. That is a consoling feeling.

**

John decides to walk to the location with a hat and sunglasses, so he will be unrecognizable. He gets to the warehouse and is able to maneuver his body over the bars of the gate, around the side of the building. He is glad he stays in shape. *There it is… the garage is not noticeable from the road.* His heart begins to race and he can feel her presence. He knows she is in there. How can he get her out? He has an idea, a very vicious, but plausible idea. He breaks into the garage and there is Maria's car. He gets out his phone and calls Jorge. "Jorge, I know where your mother is and I am leaving the office to go to the warehouse. The PI was able to track her down and I need you to meet me there to talk her into coming home with me. If she doesn't, there will be hell to pay."

Jorge immediately calls his mother to warn her and informs her she needs to immediately leave and head to his apartment. He will meet his father there to try to talk some sense into him. Maria grabs her purse, keys, and light overnight bag she has packed that has important paperwork and belongings. This is part of her safety plan… she learned while reading about escaping domestic violence. She rushes out to the garage that resembles an old barn.

It is dark so she reaches for the light switch. *The lights might be burnt out…*

From behind, a hand reaches around and covers her mouth in a death grip. "Think you could get away from me without even a goodbye, or discussion about options. Not what I deserve after taking care of you all these years." Maria's heart is pounding in her chest; a big lump choking her throat, tears welling up in her eyes.

She tells herself, N*o, you cannot go back. He cannot continue to treat you like his chattel.* She has had her friends drilling new thoughts into her head since she left. She desperately rehearses new internal dialogue and tries to wrestle free, but he has her arm turned under and the shooting pain makes her stop fighting. The old feeling of helplessness floods her. He continues to speak to her in an ominously sweet, deep, low voice.

"Maria, I need you. You cannot leave me like this… Not while I am in the middle of the campaign. It will ruin our family name. It will ruin Jorge's chances of getting into law school. The rumors… no firm would want to hire him." She feels the deep sense of guilt and fear…knowing fighting John, it is a losing prospect. She surrenders, but something inside of her has strengthened over the last several months. She unexpectedly flips her wrist, another move she read about, and John, now unsteady in his stance, trips over a rake, loosening his grip…she scurries through the bars rather than over. About that time, Jorge pulls up in his car and she rushes into his arms. Out of the garage, John is almost on all three of them. He looks like a crazed animal, and Jorge puts his mother behind him. His father lifts his fist and throws a punch at Jorge, and John lands on his back after Jorge dodged the fist and sent one of his own that landed John on his back, with a broken, bleeding nose. Jorge looks down at his father and says, "Dad, I have wanted to do that for years!"

The PI is confused; nonetheless, content finally able to finish his job. He looked down at Mr. Fisher, takes a photo and says, "I found her, just like I said I would." He turns around and walks off.

Jorge puts Maria in his truck and takes her to his apartment. John lays there with both pride and nose broken. Out of plans and most likely out of politics, if any of this gets out.

CHAPTER 24

The girls' events blur together. Sue is content to hang out with them and hear them chatter about who is who, their plans for the future, the latest trends, etc. Sue has in the back of her mind, she has not heard much from her friend, Diane. Her distrust has grown daily and she has been determined not to text or call her and see if the relationship has become more one-sided. She did hear from Jennifer that Diane was getting the cold shoulder from most of management.

It is the last night before she heads home and she has yet to clear up anything with Diane. Determined to wait until she gets to the office, but in a moment of weakness, she calls Diane. The phone rings three times and Sue feels a sense of relief, hoping she has been graced by providence to avoid the conversation, when she hears on the other end, "Hey girl, I have been busy as can be and thinking about you constantly. How are your girls doing? Man, it makes you sound like you are already a mother! ...sorry I said that... How is the pregnancy going? All is prodding along here, but I gotta admit, your job is harder than I thought. You have one loyal team. Every time, I ask them about showing me some of the details of their sales strategies, they ALL tell me, 'We can cover that with Sue when she returns.' Man, I feel like I am stomping on someone's toes, but I am not sure who?"

Finally, Sue has an opportunity to say a word, and her word is not very friendly. "Are you sure you don't know whose toes you are stepping on, or at least trying to step on?"

Diane is somewhat taken back, "What are you talking about?"

Sue responds aloof, "Some people seem to think you are trying to take my job. After all, you know I am pregnant, and the only one who knows I am pregnant. Have you told anyone, Diane?"

Diane feels a little confused. She admits to herself, she has been snooping around a bit, and considering what it would be like to be in Sue's position. She is unsure of her own motives. Part of her wants to rationalize, she is just looking at how she could step into Sue's place, if the pregnancy, God forbid, should cause the company to want to get rid of Sue. The other part, hides in the recesses of her dark mind. The part of her that has contemplated having another outing with Jack and letting it slip that she is pregnant. She does know, at this point she absolutely has not told anyone about Sue's pregnancy, so she approaches from the point of truth rather than some of the half-truths she is telling herself. "Sue, I have not told anyone about the pregnancy. I figure that will be evident soon enough and you can manage it then. As far as stepping on your toes, what do you mean?"

Sue softens a bit. She is glad no one at the office knows she is pregnant. She cannot deal with that right now. "Well, I hear through the rumor mill, you have been going above and beyond your call of duty and snooping around the office." Diane can't deny that fact, and as poorly as she has been as a best friend, she finds it difficult to lie to Sue. That is the reason; if she were honest to herself, she has not called Sue. She further distances herself from the fact she has come onto Jorge several times, to no avail. Diane begins to feel nervous, her left eye twitching. Oh no, she read somewhere, that means you are refusing to look at something clearly.

Diane, in a tone of humility and pleadingly, states, "Look Sue, I have to admit, I have been jealous of your position and how committed your team is to you. I was sort of trying to see what it might feel like to be in your position. The real reason I went out with that schmuck Jack was to see what it might take to go up the ladder. You know me; I like the idea of female persuasion as the least path of resistance. Despite him acting like a pervert most of the time, he would not take the bait, and just talked about hard work, blah blah blah. I like the sales but doing what it takes to get up the ladder is tedious."

Sue is a bit perplexed. Diane certainly is being honest, and it definitely sounds just like her. She is unsure if she should let bygones be bygones. After all, she has known Diane's character flaws for years. She just never thought she would use them on her. She is to play a little hard to get. Best friends are hard to come by and she has been a very best friend to Diane. She is not going to let her off the hook that easy. That is her hardest defect, forgiving too easily and re-engaging with those who hurt her. She has someone else to think about now. This baby is helpless and vulnerable… No one has a right to play with her financial security!!

She coldly addresses Diane, "We have been friends a long time, and friends do not treat friends like you have treated me. You are not a kid anymore… Scolding is not enough. I need to take a break for a while. We will debrief at the office when I get back and I want you to ask for a transfer, away from my team to a new manager. I do not want to have to see you daily."

Sue, feels a little shaken up by setting a boundary between her and her best friend, yet somehow feels a sense of empowerment. How seldom has she been able to stick up for herself with someone she cares about without caving when they are persistence. She wonders if she will give in, but even so, she feels she has definitely improved. Wasn't she able to do that with Jorge, too? Like a dim light bulb shining into her subconscious, slowly awakening her conscious awareness… her reality shifts. She recognizes it is not boundaries she is setting, but dividing walls. She is all or nothing, and mostly nothing. She hides behind walls and wonders why she feels so lonely so often.

She is ready to put Jerry outside of her wall. She reflects how many people she has placed outside her wall. Guilt arises, and she recognizes that villainous foe. She has read enough self-help books to feel its strangling sensations creeping up around her throat, choking her sense of value and self-trust. She asks herself some other new questions, *How many people have you let in?* She thinks of her sisters and Latisha. Really, Latisha is the only one she has been completely honest with, but they see each other so seldom. Her mind readily drifts back to the wall. She sees Jorge outside the wall and a deep sense of sadness floods her from the inside out and she grieves the fact her baby will not know her father.

She imagines her own father and she sees herself opening a gate. It is funny there is a gate to her wall. She misses her father and wonders what he may be like, if he ever thinks of her? Her head begins to hurt and she shakes away the introspection as a dog shakes off excess water from its fur.

She has to get ready and go back home, leaving early in the morning. It has been an eventful trip and her journey home is most likely anticlimactic. Her mother was able to talk her boyfriend into a private plane trip home. She must have worked her magic and fortunately, Sue can depart before her mother's arrival. She made up some excuse why she had to leave early and asked her mother if she could catch a cab from the small airport. Sue has felt unable to look her mother in the eyes… especially now… without feeling guilty about keeping her secret. Her mother always has been able to pull out of Sue any and all information she could later use against her. It is as if she has a key to her emotions and can exploit them at will.

She is leaving early enough to swing by to see Jerry, but she thinks it will be better to leave well enough alone. She is pregnant and needs to focus on her own life without making it more complicated with someone else tugging on her emotions. She dismisses the fact she allowed her thoughts to tug on heart rather than mental ascension, but only allowed it fleetingly, shoving it far from her mind. She turns out the light after the girls come in to tell her how much fun they had and can't wait until they can come and stay with her during the summer. She does not agree with it, but neither has she verbally opposed the idea. As with most teens, if you don't argue with them, they think you must be agreeing. Sue believes it is better to leave it that way then have any conflicts with them.

She can hear the rhythmic breathing of Ginger lying on the floor beside her. The girls had her sleep with them all week, but Ginger senses the time to go home and wants to make sure she is by Sue's side when she leaves. Sue can feel movement inside of her…like butterflies. The feeling is different from gas bubbles. She lays her hands on her belly and sings a lullaby she sang as a child that she still remembers.

Reflections

She sees herself walking through a fog with a dim light in front of her. She sees her five stones in the ground, shaped like a circle. The stones begin to twirl around and appear to become a wheel... a spinning wheel. Inside the wheel, she sees the face of the Indian princess, who looks sad, until the wheel attaches to a truck and the princess moves rapidly in front of the semi- truck and disappears. Sue wakes up long enough to log the dream and look it up later. She has been having these dreams too frequently to ignore them. She sits up, reaches towards the nightstand and takes out her little bag of stones. She is unsure if it is merely a coincidence there were stones and a truck in the dream, but is feeling even more longing for her father. She goes to sleep with the five stones in her hand.

Joseph has another dream, wakes up in a cold sweat. He sees the Indian Princess fighting; behind her is a basket with a child in it. The child is wailing, with big tears. The baby, wrapped in a pink blanket, is sinking in the mud like quicksand, and the warrior princess is fighting off a villainous foe. He can feel her weakening and his emotional vulnerability, as if he were the baby and the warrior princess, as well. He rouses himself out of the dream and rather than coffee, he gets his ipad.

Baby in pink blanket and basket represents happiness and security. A baby sinking in mud means fear, stress, and adversity. He realizes he is fighting for his own sense of happiness. He realizes he is afraid to look for his daughter. He believes she may reject, berate him, and shame him. The sun is peaking through the clouds and he realizes a new day has begun.

**

Joseph is up later than usual. At that moment, the phone rings and it is Jacob. Jacob can hear some distress is Joseph's voice and says, "What is wrong with you? It sounds like you had a rough night?" Joseph clears his throat but is having difficulty clearing his mind and heart. Jacob hesitates, and says, "Hey, look buddy, I know we don't know each other very well, but something seemed wrong the last time we talked… Especially when talking about my daughter Latisha. I cannot put my finger on it."

Joseph feels almost pushed internally. He has to tell someone; he is going to burst!!! He says, "I just realized she is about the same age as a person who I haven't seen in many years. It made me think of her and I guess I am dealing with some regrets.

"Believe me; I have my share of regrets. When I went to the pen, and was away from my wife and kids, I was so ashamed of myself. I thought when I got out; I would just run away from everyone." Joseph feels less guarded. He had heard Jacob went through some trouble, but didn't know he had done time. Most likely more time than the 2 weeks, he spent in jail.

"How did you move past the feeling like running away?" Joseph asks with sincerity.

"My kids, that's how. Kids are so loving and forgiving. The week before released, my girls sent me cards that said they love me and no matter what I did, I would always be their daddy. I realized at that moment, how much my kids both loved and needed me. I would just be a coward to run away."

Joseph rarely gets outwardly angry, but bursts out, "I am not a coward, but I had no choice." Before he knew he had spoken those words aloud, Jacob was trying desperately to calm Joseph.

"Hey dude, you must have misunderstood me. I didn't call you a coward. Perhaps we had a bad connection or something." Joseph, feeling like he is going a little crazy, apologizes.

Jacob tries to redirect the conversation back to his daughter in the present. I just know that broken relationships are so hard on kids. The other day my daughter met up with a friend, she has known since childhood. That little girl used to come to the house and tell me she knew if she learned about sports, when her daddy came to get her, she thought he would be proud of her. She carried this little pouch of stones with her and said she knew when she rubbed those stones, her dad would think about her."

As if life stands still, Joseph cannot speak. He cannot think. Can it be possible? How improbable? Jacob is unsure if the line might be causing trouble since he is not getting any response from Joseph. "Hey, are you there? Can you hear me?" Joseph feels urgency and the need for clarification. Joseph is unsure what to say or how to ask. It is now or never. He could let the moment go... change the subject back to business, or he could take a risk. When it came to Sue, why had he been so afraid to take risks? He realizes he needs to know. It is time to know. The Indian Princess had just given him a dream about fears, and about happiness sinking. He is certain this conversation following the dream is no coincidence.

He clears his throat, and with the uncertainty of a lost child, he asks quietly, "Was that little girl you speak of named Sue?"

Jacob, a little confused, tries to remember what else she went by. He knows Latisha met with Sue a few days back, but she always wanted Jacob to call her by another name. What was it? ...some name like Hiawatha, or Hachete? He says to Joseph, "The friend my daughter met with the other day is named Sue, why do you ask? But I remember when she would come over as a child, she always wanted me to call her Hiawatha or Hachete, or some Indian sort of name...said it made her feel close to her dad."

Joseph gasps for air. The world closes in on him and he feels dizzy and almost faint. He grabs onto the nightstand next to him to steady himself. He almost knocks the lamp over and notices his bag of stones has spilled open and the one with a pink tone seems to be almost translucent. Jacob, again, is unsure about what is transpiring on the other end of the phone. He is beginning to have some doubts about collaborating with someone who seems so flaky and unstable. He is about to pardon himself from the conversation when Joseph gets the wherewithal to speak.

"Jacob, I think you are talking about my daughter that I abandoned 15 or more years ago."

There is silence on the other end, and Jacob feels his blood flowing and his anger rising. He remembers the deep sadness and loneliness in that little girl's eyes. He remembers all the times she talked about her father coming to pick her up in his truck. Yes, sounds like this is the loser that let his daughter live with such a mean mother. All of the kids knew how mean Samantha was. He loses control and blurts out, "You selfish son of a bitch. How do you call yourself a man and crush the heart of such a precious little girl? I can't tell you how many times she sat by me with big alligator tears in her eyes, waiting for her daddy. I should beat your white ass, but I don't want to go back to the pen. You can forget doing any sort of partnership with you. Don't call me back. It is an insult to think we are on the same playing field about to be grandfathers. You should never have such a privilege... a right to break another kid's heart. You can take those tracking systems and shove them up your ass. Maybe then your daughter could track down your sorry ass." CLICK...

Before he can clearly get a grasp on whether or not his daughter is alive and well. ...before he can ask her whereabouts, the phone disconnected. Joseph is stunned. Slapped across the face with the truth; he is a coward, a son of a bitch. He has been selfish to let so much time go by. He has to face this to get past it. *Face your greatest fear. Isn't that what I teach my drivers to build their confidence? ...visualize disasters and determine how to manage them.* Why could he have not lived by the same principles? *What did Jacob mean about both being grandfathers? Was he speaking of potentially being a grandfather?* About the time, he dives into reflection, his phone rings. Hoping it will be Jacob, he picks it up quickly and it is Jeff. He calls to let him know he received an email from Jacob stating, 'For personal reasons, I am withdrawing my business partnership plan. Best Regards. This email does not require a response.'

Back to his same old defenses, when Jeff asks him what is wrong, he just replies, "It is probably for the best. The last time we spoke, we had some significant differences. I was sort of expecting it. No big deal." Jeff shrugs it off knowing ultimately Joseph prefers to be a loner and some things never change.

CHAPTER 25

Jorge sits on his bar stool drinking fresh espresso made by his mother. She has been at his apartment the past couple of days until the divorce process is secure enough. She realizes she does not want to live in that house where she suffered so much and wants to make sure the restraining order is in place at her work before she returns. She took a five day much needed break. Sue's attorney contacted by John's firm, requests a legal separation if feasible… since it would look better on the firm and John's campaign. She is surprised he is continuing with the political career, but then again, without her and Jorge, whom else does he have to dominate except the world at large. Maria notices Jorge has been quiet since the incident. She thinks it might be a good time to put in some good words for Sarah.

"You know Jorge; Sarah is such a beautiful young lady. She works so diligently and is full of faith. I was just hoping you might like to ask her out. Not that she has really said anything about it, but you are so charming, I am sure you could coax her away from her work. I saw how you looked at her when you were with her. I know you found her muy bonita?"

Jorge, glances out the kitchen window, with some nostalgic sentiment, "Si madre, ella es bonita, pero hay otra señorita que me gusta más." His mother sees a look in her son she has no recollection of ever seeing before. "How come you have never mentioned her? What is her name and where did you meet?"

Jorge looks at his mother and says, "Mom, I think it is too late. I started treating her as Dad treated you. In fact, I have treated all my women that way. She pulls away and won't let me talk to her. She hangs up or does not answer her phone. She does not want to ever see me again, but I cannot get her out of my mind." Maria is somewhat unsure about her son. She has seen some of his disposition, and as much as she loves him, she is fearful he has more of her husband's traits than she has wanted to admit.

"Jorge, could it be you want her because she doesn't want you? Sort of like playing football and trying to get the fumble? I just want you to consider that. I think your father really didn't love me, but he just didn't want anyone else to want me. He always wants what he cannot have."

In all honesty, Jorge has pondered those very thoughts, and if fact, at first, it was really about what he couldn't have. Nevertheless, when he saw himself pulling away from Diane, and realized he really didn't want to hurt Sue by being with her best friend, he reflected more about his feelings. He responds to his mother, "When you told me I should treat a woman like a beautiful rose, the first person I ever wanted to treat that way is Sue. The problem is, I never had a chance to do that. I don't know what else to do."

Maria enjoys philosophical ideas, states, "Let her go, and if she is meant to be with you, it will happen."

Jorge couldn't help but burst into laughter. "Mom, you know I cannot keep myself from some sort of definitive action. Remember, that is how I was raised!" Maria couldn't deny that, so she just smiled. It is at least nice to know her son is reflecting on how to love. Whether he can actually do it is yet to be seen.

He throws on his dress clothes for work and gives his mother a kiss on the cheek. "Don't keep rearranging things in the apartment. Maybe you should get out and go see grandpa. I am sure he is wondering what in the heck has happened to you." He chugs down the last bit of espresso and puts the blue cup in the sink, leaving Maria little time to determine her day. She has worked so hard the past few years just to stay away from John and feel some sense of importance, other than work and housekeeping, she had let go of most of her outside socialization, including her family. She does not want her father to see the bruises and John always found reasons to convince her to stay away from her family.

She knows if she tells her parents she is getting a divorce, they will be very disappointed. Disappointed not only because of their Catholic beliefs about marriage 'til death do you part', even if it means your own death, but also because John had filled them with high hopes on his immigration ideals. She decides to go to the mall and just become invisible with the crowds. She knows she wants to redecorate her new house or apartment, so she could get some ideas. She is tired of coming up with decorating ideas, and would like to get a fresh perspective. She decides to wear some white pants, and a sheer low cut blouse. She puts on a chic white sunhat and sunglasses. This look is not her… no one will notice her.

She pulls into the parking lot and decides she is little hungry. She never ate breakfast and it is past noon. She gets into the mall and heads towards the food court. While looking at all the various foods, she decides on something simple, like a submarine sandwich… both low calorie and filling. She sits down on a bench next to the fountain waiting for her order and notices a woman wrestling with her bags, purse, and food. She is unsure whether the young woman is pregnant, but she sort of has that glow and a little bit of a pooch. She certainly understands with today's' society, one never knows when a person may just be a little chubby and wearing looser clothing. She decides she should help this woman before she spills her drink all over. She jumps over just in time to catch the drink from spilling and with her motherly instinct; she grabs her bag of food, holds her arm, and leads her over to where she is sitting. Before the young woman can object, she is sitting next to this kind and attractive Hispanic female.

Maria introduces herself. "Hello, my name is Maria, and I am so sorry I just grabbed you like I did. I just didn't want you to spill your drink all over your packages."

"Hello Maria, my name is Sue and I appreciate you helping me with everything. It seems often in life; I bite off more than I can chew. I was trying to juggle too much."

They sit there and eat their lunch talking small talk and Maria notices a pink teddy bear in one of Sue's bags. She uses this as an opportunity to snoop a little. "Is this for some pretty little girl's birthday? It is such a cute pink bear. I always wanted a girl, but I lost my girl in a miscarriage and then couldn't have any more children than my one son." Sue feels a small heart pain as reminded of how quickly she is attached to little one.

Sue responds, "No, I am pregnant, and just have the feeling it is a girl. I thought it would be nice to begin to prepare."

"How excited the father must be? You both must be thrilled." Sue is hesitant, and a little embarrassed, but says candidly, "No, the father doesn't really know. He just dropped out of the picture. It is probably better. He was really sort of a jerk... You know... kind of a control freak. Not what any kid needs to grow up... My mother was enough of a control freak; I certainly would have hated to have grown up with a father that way." Sue catches herself and feels a little uneasy about disclosing so much. She has the urge to leave, and besides, she has to pee and that is a good excuse to go. "It was nice to meet you Maria. I have the pregnancy urge to urinate, if you know what I mean, so I have to run." Leaving half a sandwich, and her lemonade sitting there, Maria sits there thinking about what it would have been like if her baby had lived, and if she had been with some other man, besides John.

Sue left her apartment in a mess so she goes home to feed Ginger. She did not want to be by herself after having so much time with her sisters, and left alone with thoughts of work and Diane…. thoughts about Jorge or Jerry. All of this was too much to be on her mind. She had thought going to the mall would get her mind off her ruminations, only to run into that woman Maria, who stirred up more thoughts about Jorge. She does like Jerry, and he seems to be a lot like her, taking care of his siblings, working all the time. Besides that, Ginger really likes him and he lives far enough away, she can keep in touch and maybe go out when she visits her sisters. *Who is she kidding? A three or four hour away relationship and a baby on top… Bad idea…* Then there are the thoughts of Jorge and him not knowing of the baby. No, she just couldn't bring herself to do it. She would not have a control freak involved with her and her baby. Ultimately, her thoughts and heart never leave very far from her stones in her pocket… and father. As mad as she should be, she just cannot feel angry with him. She knows her mother well and understands she probably holds something over his head. She instinctively is aware as a little child that her mother was jealous over her and her father's relationship. She hopes she is not afraid of this with this baby and that is why she has not been willing to tell Jorge. *Is she going to create in her child the same agony of an absent father?*

Sue arrives at her apartment only to find her worst nightmare. There sits Jorge waiting on her. *What is he doing here?* She defensively looks down at her stomach and covers it with her purse to make sure he cannot tell she is pregnant. She does not go much closer, but in a raised voice, says, "Jorge, you need to leave. Obviously I have not returned your calls for a reason."

He walks around his car and very unexpectedly, he gets down on his knees and says, "Sue, I have been an ass, I have been controlling, self-centered, and inconsiderate. I have missed you and my ego has been bigger than my heart. Please forgive me. I will not pressure you. I just want to let you know, and if you ever decide to give me a second chance, I will try hard. I don't want to end up like my dad… a lonely, wealthy, rigid, controlling and miserable old man." He walks back around his car, gets in, and leaves.

Sue stands there with her mouth open. She is ready for a rebuttal, but who can rebut an admission of character defect and an apology. Wow, life is full of the unexpected. Her black and white thinking has definitely fallen in the mud and is now a murky grey. She cannot go back into the apartment yet. Now more cluttered than ever, she decides to go to the park and despite being pregnant, take a little jog. She cannot even muster up the strength to go in and get Ginger to go with her. Her emotions are shot. She puts her purse and bags in the trunk, and her keys in her sweatpants. Off she goes, mindlessly looking at the trees and sees a squirrel as she runs past the entrance to the park. She loves this park because of the lake near the jogging trail. She takes a slow pace and gets winded faster than usual. It has been awhile since she has jogged and her legs and joints feel different. The doctor told her she can continue with any activity she has been used to. She has regularly jogged for several years.

She didn't think a week or two would make a difference. The doctor said she is now 13 weeks and will definitely feel the baby in a couple of weeks. She is sure she has felt her already. She told her doctor she did not need to know the sex of the baby. Truth is, she already knows she is a girl. She has felt her and most of all seen her in her dreams, seen her with the Indian princess. One of these days, she is going to do some genealogy to find out more about her father's family history. She is convinced this aberration is a relative visiting her; and she has some unresolved issues of her own… but right now, she is not in a position to help an ancestral ghost… *Maybe one day…*

Short of breath, she leans over, right on the edge of the lake. She looks down and begins to gaze at the small stones by the lake. She reaches in her pocket for a small pouch. Sitting nearby, on a bench, a desperate and agonized man observes her and notices she takes out a small leather pouch. This day has been much too bizarre for him. He stirs up what little courage lays in him, and walks in her direction. She is busy looking over a variety of stones; her hair is up in a weathered and wind-blown ponytail. He notices her skin is an olive tan color. He looks at his own skin and recognizes the similarities. He sees her profile and it reminds him of someone he has seen before. He continues to move forward, and before he can add logic to heart, he speaks aloud, "Hachi?"

Without thought, she quickly glances up, startled to hear such a name. As she rises from a crouched position, she slowly moves around and sees a handsome older man, gazing deeply in her eyes. She notices his hair in a long braid down his back. Before he can say a word, he reaches into his pocket and pulls out his leather pouch. As if the world has turned to slow motion, she runs and leaps into his arms. The strength of a young warrior enters his body, and he lifts her up in the air.

He slowly brings her down to look her in her eyes, and lifts his bag. "I never forgot."

She lifts her bag… "And I never stopped waiting." As they gaze into each other's eyes, the wind rustles in the trees as the Indian Princess smiles and blows down love and forgiveness. Little one twirls around with delight…

The End, or is it?

The beginning…